DEVELOPING CREATIVITY IN ORGANIZATIONS

Michael A. West

Personal and Professional Development

DEVELOPING CREATIVITY
IN ORGANIZATIONS

Michael A. West

Professor of Work and Organizational Psychology
Institute of Work Psychology
University of Sheffield, UK

BPS
BOOKS Published by The British Psychological Society

First published in 1997 by BPS Books (The British Psychological Society), St Andrews House, 48 Princess Road East, Leicester LE1 7DR, UK, and 22883 Quicksilver Drive, Stirling, VA 20166, USA.

A catalogue record for this book is available from the British Library. Library of Congress Cataloging-in-Publication Data on file.

ISBN 1 85433 229 5

Typeset by HouseStyle Graphics, Clerkenwell Road, London EC1M 5PS
Printed in Great Britain by Biddles Ltd, Guildford, Surrey GU1 1DA.

Whilst every effort has been made to ensure the accuracy of the contents of this publication, the publishers and authors expressly disclaim responsibility in law for negligence or any other cause of action whatsoever.

OTHER TITLES IN THE SERIES:
Assessing Your Career: Time for Change? by Ben Ball
Basic Evaluation Methods by Glynis Breakwell and Lynne Millward
Coaching for Staff Development by Angela Thomas
Coping with Aggressive Behaviour by Glynis Breakwell
Effective Teamwork by Michael West
Interpersonal Conflicts at Work by Robert Edelmann
Managing Time by David Fontana
Teaching and Training for Non-Teachers by Derek Milne and Steve Noone

Personal and Professional Development

SERIES EDITORS:
Glynis M. Breakwell is Professor of Psychology and Pro-Vice-Chancellor of the University of Surrey, UK.

David Fontana is Reader in Educational Psychology at the University of Wales College of Cardiff, and Professor Catedrático, University of Minho, Portugal.

The books in this series are designed to help readers use psychological insights, theories and methods to address issues which arise regularly in their own personal and professional lives and which affect how they manage their jobs and careers. Psychologists have a great deal to say about how to improve our work styles. The emphasis in this series is upon presenting psychology in a way which is easily understood and usable. We are committed to enabling our readers to use psychology, applying it for themselves to themselves.

The books adopt a highly practical approach. Readers are confronted with examples and exercises which require them to analyse their own situation and review carefully what they think, feel and do. Such analyses are necessary precursors in coming to an understanding of where and what changes are needed, or can reasonably be made.

These books do not reflect any single approach in psychology. The editors come from different branches of the discipline. They work together with the authors to ensure that each book provides a fair and comprehensive review of the psychology relevant to the issues discussed.

Each book deals with a clearly defined target and can stand alone. But combined they form an integrated and broad resource, making wide areas of psychological expertise more freely accessible.

ACKNOWLEDGEMENTS

I am grateful to a number of people with whom I have studied innovation. In particular, Neil Anderson, David Bunce, James Farr, Lynn Markiewicz, Richard Mindell, Nigel Nicholson and Peter Wallach have been stimulating, creative and productive colleagues whose ideas and support have influenced my thinking about creativity and innovation. I thank you. My thanks go also to Angela Waddams for preparing the manuscript with care and professionalism.

The Bushmen, who walk immense distances across the Kalahari, have no idea of the soul's survival in another world. 'When we die, we die', they say. 'The wind blows out our footprints, and that is the end of us.

Bruce Chatwin, *The Songlines*

Contents

DEDICATION

To my mother, M. Joyce Owen, from whom I learned that creativity
and persistence are at the root of innovation.

Chapter One

Creativity and Innovation at Work

We cannot wait for great visions from great people, for they are in short supply… It is up to us to light our own small fires in the darkness.
Charles Handy

Employees frequently have ideas for improving their workplaces, work functioning, processes, products or services and those around them have considerable influence in encouraging or hindering this creativity. Indeed, organizations create an ethos or atmosphere within which creativity is either nurtured and blooms in innovation or is starved of the oxygen of support which enables growth. This book will explore ways of developing creativity and innovation in work organizations, beginning at the level of individuals, moving on to groups or teams at work, and then describing organizational innovation. The aim is to help people at work develop their skills in building work environments which will release and guide their creative energy and the energy of those with whom they work.

In this chapter we begin by examining what is meant by creativity and innovation and what the distinctions are between these two. Then, we look at two case studies of organizations and ask whether innovation is simply another management fad, and creativity merely the accompanying costume jewellery. Finally, we ask which factors encourage innovation in organizations, as a prelude to the in-depth examination of these issues in the following chapters.

WHAT IS CREATIVITY?

Creativity is the bringing together of knowledge from different areas of experience to produce new and improved ideas. Creativity is *not* something limited to a chosen few – to artists, composers and scientific geniuses. It is a fundamental part of being human. All of us are naturally creative and invent new approaches to problems as we go about our daily lives. Small children with their immense powers of imagination prove this beyond a doubt. Creativity involves us in the constant discovery of new and improved ways of doing things; it means challenging well-tried and traditional approaches and coping with the conflict and change which this inevitably causes. Creativity is discovering the elegant patterns of meaning across diverse areas of our knowledge and experience.

A more scientific definition is that '*Creativity is a context specific, subjective judgement of the novelty and value of an outcome of an individual's or a collective's behavior*' (Ford, 1995). Ford's definition implies that defining what is creative is dependent upon the context in which an idea, process, product or procedure is offered. So if the concern of readers of this book is with creativity within organizations, then creative ideas have to be judged within the context of organizational settings. If their concern is with art or music, then judgements are best made by experts in these domains. At the same time, Ford argues that creativity is a *subjective* judgement of novelty and value – it is not something that can be objectively determined, like height or weight. So Ford argues that we should define creativity in terms of judgements made by people who are familiar with a particular organizational context or profession, and that we should also determine creativity by the extent to which these judges agree that a particular idea is both new and potentially useful. Finally, he argues that creativity refers to an *outcome* produced by an individual, group or organization. This final point merely confirms that creativity is not something that lives *within* individuals, but is something that is judged on the external manifestation of ideas they produce or processes that they generate and that are publicly observable.

Creativity is an intensely subjective concept with which psychologists have grappled for over a hundred years as they have attempted to judge the creativity of individuals, products, ideas and processes. This fascination derives from a recognition that creativity is a potent element of individual life experience and is the soil at the root of much of human progress and endeavour.

There has been considerable discussion and debate about whether creativity should be seen primarily as residing in people's cognitive processes, that is, in the way that thoughts and ideas are managed to produce creative ideas; creativity as being vested in products, for example, a creative cave painting or a creative piece of music; or creativity as a largely inherited personality trait, evidenced in a highly creative scientist, musician or architect. In the next chapter we will examine what types of cognitive processes, personal characteristics and work environments are associated with creativity. For now we will move on to examine the related concept of innovation.

WHAT IS INNOVATION?

If creativity is the development of new ideas, innovation is the process of actually putting them into practice. Perhaps the biggest challenge for creative people is persuading others to accept their ideas and then to be successful in implementing them in the workplace. Not surprisingly therefore, the topic of innovation has generated enormous interest and research activity in a variety of disciplines over many years. Sociologists, psychologists, economists, policy makers, managers and organizational scientists have struggled to understand the factors which determine innovation in organizations and also to understand how innovations may be managed over time. This extraordinarily wide interest in innovation continues and, if anything, is increasing. Throughout the industrial world, there is great emphasis by central government, managers and policy makers upon the topic of innovation. The increasingly vigorous competition in global markets requires that organizations innovate and adapt if they are to survive and compete effectively in their environments. Indeed, vast amounts of money are now being invested by governments in order to promote understanding of innovation within organizations.

Innovation is the introduction of new and improved ways of doing things at work. This is a definition at its simplest. A more psychological or complex definition of innovation is that it is the *intentional introduction and application within a job, work team or organization of ideas, processes, products or procedures which are new to that job, work team or organization and which are designed to benefit the job, the work team or the organization.* Innovation is restricted to *intentional* attempts to bring about benefits from new changes; these might include economic benefits, personal growth, increased satisfaction, improved group cohesiveness, better organizational communication, as well as the productivity and economic measures that we usually consider. Innovations may include technological changes such as new products, but may also include new production processes, the introduction of advanced manufacturing technology or the introduction of new computer support services within an organization. Innovations may also be found in administrative changes. New human resource management (HRM) strategies, organizational policies or the intro-duction of teamwork are all examples of administrative innovations within organizations.

Innovation does not imply absolute novelty. Change can be deemed an innovation if it is new for the person, group or organiza-tion which is introducing it. If teamwork is introduced into a govern-ment department, it is considered to be an innovation if it is new in that government department, irrespective of whether it has been introduced into other government departments.

Of course, innovations may vary from those which are relatively minor to those which are of great significance. Innovation does not necessarily mean inventing the equivalent of the internal combus-tion engine! It is *any* new and improved product or way of doing things which an individual, group or organization has introduced and which affects individuals, jobs, groups or organizations. Some innovations can be introduced in the space of an hour (for example, deciding to set up a new computerized diary system), while others may take several years, as in the case of British Petroleum attempting to change its corporate culture in the 1990s. Some innovations are unplanned and emerge by accident. A recent drought in England led many companies to find innovative ways of conserving water supplies which have been maintained even though the drought has receded. But many innovations are planned and managed, requiring an enormous amount of an organization's attention and energy in order to ensure their effective implementation.

Overall, therefore, in this book we shall regard creativity as the generation of ideas for new and improved ways of doing things at work and innovation as the implementation of those ideas in practice.

❏ Case Study: The Energy of Innovative Organizations
As part of a major research project on corporate performance, I visited a wire and cable company and spent the day interviewing senior managers and touring the manufacturing plant learning about its operations. This company operates in a highly competitive market but its market share is growing. At the end of nine hours of interviewing, I left exhausted and somewhat anxious that I had gathered too little information. The next day I visited another company, which manufactures UPVC windows. Again I interviewed senior managers and spent some time watching the production

process. This company also has a market share which is growing, despite the fact that it is in a highly competitive environment. After four hours of relatively relaxed discussions with senior management and a tour of the shop floor, I left feeling I had gathered all of the information I needed. I also felt that the second company – the window manufacturers – was much less likely to be in business in ten years' time than the first company. The reason for this is that the wire and cable company is innovating in almost every area of its operations while the window manufacturer only makes changes when competitors develop a new fitting or design which threatens their market position.

The reason why the difference in length of interview time was so great between these two companies was because the wire and cable company was busy developing new ways of doing things, and employers and employees were so enthusiastic and eager to talk about these that there was an enormous amount of information to absorb. In contrast, in the UPVC window company, shop floor employees had been deskilled; each worked on a strict job cycle time of two minutes thirty seconds, and the company had little or no strategy for training, human resource management, quality control, communication or teamwork. Consequently, only the senior managers had much information to offer about the company. Nevertheless, the company is efficient and doing well financially. However, the problem for this company is that their highly efficient operation is readily imitated by others in the industry. Indeed, their own strategy of innovating only in response to competitors' new ideas demonstrates this neatly.

INNOVATION AND PERFORMANCE

Does innovation lead to better economic performance? The work of economists demonstrates clearly that there is a consistent and positive relationship between levels of company innovation and their financial performance. Most commentators now also believe that if companies in any sector are to remain competitive they must develop innovative strategies. However, research has demonstrated that the extent of innovation in many organizations is low – most innovations are relatively small scale, having little impact on business and there is often considerable resistance to change (Pillinger and West, 1995). For example, in the UPVC window company described in the case study, the major innovation over the previous two years had been the board's approval of a management development centre programme, though it had not been implemented.

WHAT STIMULATES INNOVATION?

● A major determinant of innovation is challenge in the organization's environment. For example, manufacturing companies with low market share are more likely to innovate, as is the case with both the window and the wire and cable companies, though their styles of innovating are very different. For the window company, innovation is a reactive, knee jerk strategy. When competitors do something new, they simply copy them. In the wire and cable company, innovation is the fabric of the organization. New and improved products, processes and procedures are springing up everywhere. But in both organizations innovation is often a response to challenges in their environments. Necessity is certainly a stimulus to innovation, if not its parent.

● Innovative organizations place strong emphasis on quality, but quality checks do not just occur at the end of the production or service process. In the wire and cable company, evidence of a concern with quality is everywhere, with sophisticated mechanisms for giving all employees information about their work. Moreover, this information is visible and widely shared.

● Companies which have introduced and developed effective teamwork are much more likely to be innovating. In the wire and cable company, 100 per cent of employees work in one or more teams; these are real teams, with clear shared objectives and regular team meetings. All employees receive at least one week of training on working in teams every year and cross-functional and project improvement teams are widespread throughout the organization. Most importantly they are busy, vigorously debating issues and challenging management assumptions.

● Interdepartmental communication and co-ordination are important determinants of innovation enabled by carefully designed procedures for ensuring effective joint working. In the wire and cable company, the inevitable conflicts between departments are worked out in vigorous and open ways within cross-functional teams.

● Communication in organizations also has a major impact on innovations. The wire and cable company places enormous emphasis on communication, with a company newspaper issued regularly, team briefings weekly and the use of teams to generate information and opinion flow in every direction.

• Managerial support for innovation is crucial if people are to develop and implement ideas for new and improved ways of doing things. There is enormous support for innovation in the wire and cable company, wherever ideas come from. The company had set up a team to focus on promoting creativity and innovation and they have a radical business process re-engineering plan to cut product lead time (from the time of receiving an order for a product to sending it to the customer) by a factor of four in the coming year. But the innovation is not all major and sensational. On one section of the shop floor are lots of broomheads like upturned moustaches on top of the advanced technology. We discovered that one of the operators had the idea that multiple wet cables could run separately and smoothly across the heads of the brushes while being partially dried in the process. The system works perfectly and saves the company unnecessarily costly high technology solutions to their problems of materials flow.

• The most innovative organizations are those where fundamental assumptions are open for question. Within and across teams in innovative organizations there is a questioning of objectives, strategies and processes in the challenge to find new and better ways of doing things. There is reflection, debate, constructive conflict and open disagreement which is seen as helpful rather than negative. This helps to ensure that innovation does not become an end in itself but is a means to improve products, processes and procedures, and that change is seen as appropriate.

• Participation and employee involvement are characteristic of the most innovative organizations. Another difference between the two companies described in the case study was that in the window company as I toured the shop floor, the manager showing me around only occasionally spoke to the operators and not on first name terms. In the wire and cable company there were more such interactions, but I noticed that, unusually, it was often the operators who were first to start conversations with managers about production processes, problems and successes, and always on first name terms. The sense of participation and mutual respect was tangible.

Among the four themes which these two case studies draw out, the first is that creativity and innovation are not 'add-ons'. Innovation and creativity must represent central elements in a coherent organizational strategy. Companies have to work hard and consistently to create the right conditions for thriving innovation by fostering teamwork, working constantly to emphasize quality and encouraging clear and open communication in all directions. This can take a long period of time and requires a sustained and intelligent strategy to bring about change. Second, innovation produces conflicts since it requires changing the status quo. But healthy conflict generates innovation and change. Third, innovation is limited if it is simply used as a reactive strategy as in the case in the window company. Too many organizations attempt to play 'catch up' in this way or rely on knee jerk reactions to competition. To remain competitive, companies must develop pro-active and long term strategies of developing new and improved ways of doing things in every area of their operations. This is innovating for success rather than innovating merely for *survival.* Fourth, at the root of organizational innovation is individual creativity. It is *people* who develop ideas and have the courage to propose, support and implement them in the face of inevitable resistance among their colleagues.

CHAPTER SUMMARY

These four themes – the importance of individual creativity, strategies for innovation, recognition that innovation is a product of constructive conflict, and the importance of pro-active approaches to innovation – are fundamental to the structure of this book. To develop creativity and innovation in organizations means to adopt a pro-active, planned strategy and to put effort into the processes of creativity and innovation. It means attracting, developing and enhancing the creativity of people who work within organizations. It also means encouraging constructive conflict and diversity of views within modern heterogeneous organizations in order to generate the rich mix of perspectives which produce creative ideas and innovation. Above all, it requires an orientation, amongst individuals, groups, and organizations as a whole, of experimentation, risk taking, creating and meeting challenges, and encouraging human growth and creativity.

In the following chapters, we will explore a number of domains of creativity and innovation:

- confidence in creativity and developing individual creativity at work;
- implementing individual creativity and innovation in the workplace;

- creativity and innovation in work teams;
- developing organizational innovativeness;
- managing the process of innovation in organizations;
- an overall strategy for innovations in organizations.

Chapter Two

Confidence in Creativity

It may be that when we no longer know what to do, we have come to our real work, and when we no longer know which way to go, we have begun our real journey.
Wendell Barry

Developing creativity and innovation at work begins with developing the creativity of individuals; new ideas come from the motivation, thinking and experimentation of people in their workplaces. To some extent this is influenced by the nature of their job and of the organization, but the starting place is nevertheless the individual. In this chapter we will look at:

- how to develop confidence in creativity;
- how to develop the skills and characteristics of creative people;
- which work environments aid individual creativity;
- how to practise the skills of creativity;
- when to exercise creative abilities.

Recently I worked with 120 Masters of Business Administration (MBA) students at the Graduate School of Management at the University of Queensland in Australia, exploring the nature of lateral thinking and the students' own creative abilities. This group of people represented some of the cream of academic and work organizations in Queensland and varied in age from 20- to 40-years-old. They had, by virtue of their being accepted on to the course, achieved very good academic qualifications. In most cases they had acquired prestigious jobs within leading organizations and had a commitment to developing their academic and practical skills in business administration. They were asked to rate their own individual creativity on a scale ranging from 1 'Not at all creative' to 10 'Very highly creative'. Given the abilities of this group of people it would expected that the average rating would be somewhere around 8 to 9 with a sprinkling of 10s and very few low scores. In fact, in this group, as in every group with whom I have worked, people rated themselves as moderately high, or more usually only average, or moderately low. A handful scored in the area of 8 or 9, but most rated themselves at about 5, 6 or 7. This is clearly an inappropriate self-attribution, given the likelihood that these people were highly creative individuals with a great deal to contribute in terms of creative problem identification and problem-solving. One of the most important contributors, if not *the* most important contributor, to individual creativity at work is the confidence, or sense of efficacy, of the individual in her or his own creative abilities.

When we lack confidence in our own abilities, challenges become threats and change is to be avoided and resisted rather than welcomed. Low confidence inhibits creativity. One of the reasons that human beings have become a temporarily dominant species on this planet is because we are extraordinarily creative. We have the capacity to adapt to and change our environments in ever new and different ways. Although there are some small differences in creativity between people, the fact remains that each of us is highly creative. In order to use that creativity at work, it is necessary to 'own' our own creativity; to recognize the various areas of our lives in which we are creative; and, above all, to be confident in our creative ability. This is often inhibited or reduced by our experiences in educational systems and organizations which tend inappropriately to devalue creative expression in favour of convergent or closed thinking. *Exercise 1* describes activities which can strengthen confidence in creativity, and gives you, the reader, the opportunity to judge how frequently you engage in such activities. Then you can consider how you can increase these activities to develop greater confidence in your creativity. *Exercise 2* offers a simple way of becoming aware of the scope and intensity of your creative expression in everyday life.

CONFIDENCE IN CREATIVITY

EXERCISE 1

Below is a list of activities which can help to generate confidence and boost creativity. Consider the list carefully and indicate how frequently you engage in each of the following activities:

	Almost never	Infrequently	Moderately often	Very frequently	All of the time
1. Relax in dealing with problems	1	2	3	4	5
2. Let one answer lead to another	1	2	3	4	5
3. Break away from the obvious, the commonplace	1	2	3	4	5
4. Defer judgements of my own ideas	1	2	3	4	5
5. Generate multiple solutions	1	2	3	4	5
6. Give myself time to consider problems	1	2	3	4	5
7. Trust my own wisdom	1	2	3	4	5
8. Review my strengths and skills	1	2	3	4	5
9. Reject negative self statements (for example, 'I can't do it')	1	2	3	4	5
10. Give myself space to create ideas	1	2	3	4	5
11. Take relaxation breaks – go for walks and get fresh air	1	2	3	4	5
12. Try to develop new ideas in a pleasant environment	1	2	3	4	5
13. Get away from interruptions	1	2	3	4	5
14. Use humour to ease tension and generate ideas	1	2	3	4	5

continued

continued

	Almost never	Infre-quently	Moder-ately often	Very fre-quently	All of the time
15. Build confidence by seeking out information	1	2	3	4	5
16. Break tasks into manageable parts	1	2	3	4	5
17. Avoid working with negative people while developing ideas	1	2	3	4	5
18. Develop a self image of being a creative person	1	2	3	4	5
19. Apply strengths, skills and creativity in other areas of life to the task area	1	2	3	4	5
20. Make the challenge fun rather than a threat	1	2	3	4	5
21. Forget practicalities	1	2	3	4	5
22. Let go	1	2	3	4	5
23. See things in new ways	1	2	3	4	5
24. Be playful	1	2	3	4	5
25. Avoid thinking 'I'm not creative'	1	2	3	4	5
26. Have the courage of my convictions in the face of opposition	1	2	3	4	5

Once you have rated yourself in relation to each of these ways of generating confidence in creativity, note the areas where you almost never, or only rarely, behave in ways which generate confidence, and think about how you could increase your abilities in this.

CREATIVE CHECKLIST

EXERCISE 2

Consider all the ways in which you engage in creative activity in your life. Put a tick against any activity which you do (even if only occasionally), and which involves some creativity. At the end of the list add at least four other activities which involve you in creative expression from time to time. Remember that false modesty can lead to inaccurate self-understanding and lack of confidence about creativity. Tick boxes opposite activities even where you are only occasionally creative. In this way you will become aware of the variety of your creative expression.

Gardening ☐
Singing ☐
Cooking ☐
Planning holidays ☐
Caring for those you love ☐
Playing with children ☐
Car maintenance ☐
Writing letters ☐
Choosing clothes ☐
Weekend activities ☐
Playing music ☐
Daily dressing ☐
Making clothes ☐
Negotiating ☐
Flower arranging ☐
Writing poetry or stories ☐
Writing reports ☐
Socializing ☐
House maintenance ☐
Playing sport ☐

CHARACTERISTICS OF CREATIVE PEOPLE

One way of developing confidence in creativity is to develop a number of personal qualities that have been identified repeatedly as characteristic of those who are consistently creative (see *Figure 1*). These include the following:

- *Intellectual and artistic values*
  Those who are consistently creative in their work tend to be attracted to intellectual pursuits such as high quality reading, philosophy, science and mathematics. They are also often interested in grappling with philosophical, political and human problems. They frequently have well-developed artistic values, including an appreciation of art, music, writing, dance, literature, cinema and theatre. Sometimes, stretching our exposure to new areas of reading, thinking, art, music and science can foster much greater creativity within us.

- *Attraction to complexity*
  They tend to be people who are interested in exploring complex, difficult issues in order either to understand them more fully or else to generate solutions to those problems.

- *Concern with work and achievement*
  Creative people tend to be self-disciplined in matters concerning work, with a high degree of drive and motivation and a concern with achieving excellence. They tend to be self-motivated and derive particular pleasure from achieving effectively in the work place.

- *Perseverance*
  The most creative people tend to have an obstinate determination to achieve their goals and to identify and solve problems in the work place, often in the face of frustration and obstacles. They often have a belief in their own strengths and skills which justifies their perseverance. *Exercise 3* describes a straightforward way of increasing confidence in strengths and skills which can then motivate perseverance.

- *Independence of judgement*
  While many of us have a tendency to conform to the views expressed by the majority or by those in superior positions, creative and innovative people display a characteristic independence in coming to their own conclusions, and then remaining loyal to their opinions and attitudes.

- *Tolerance of ambiguity*
  People tend to feel some discomfort in situations which are uncertain and ambiguous. For example, the experience of arriving in a foreign country and being unclear about the appropriate rules and behavioural norms can be unsettling. Creative people often respond positively to such ambiguous situations, enjoying the process of sense making.

- *Need for autonomy*
  Creative people tend to be self-directed and less dependent on others, enjoying and requiring freedom in their work. They have a high need for freedom, control and discretion in the work place and often find bureaucratic limitations or the exercise of control by managers very frustrating.

- *Self-confidence*
  An important characteristic which we have already considered in relation to the personal characteristics of creative people is a confidence in themselves and the nourishing of a creative self-image. People who believe in their own creativity and are confident of their abilities are more likely to behave creatively in the workplace.

- *An orientation towards risk-taking*
  Again, not surprisingly, those who are more creative at work tend to be more prepared to take risks with new ideas and to try new and improved ways of doing things, even when those around them may not be supportive. They are prepared to bring about change in their pursuit of improved performance and task excellence at work.

Of course, people are creative without their personalities matching this list of characteristics – what is important is confidence and valuing and encouraging these positive traits in ourselves. Consider developing self-discipline in work in order to persevere in the face of frustration; developing independence of judgement regardless of the groups or individuals we find ourselves with; learning to stay with problems; suspending judgement and keeping response options open; learning to tolerate ambiguity and increasing our own independence and autonomy within the workplace in order to release creative potential. Taking carefully controlled risks in the workplace can build the personal characteristics associated with creativity. Increasing the autonomy we have in carrying out work can be achieved by taking on more responsibility, persistently asking for permission to take risks and seeking the support of administrative

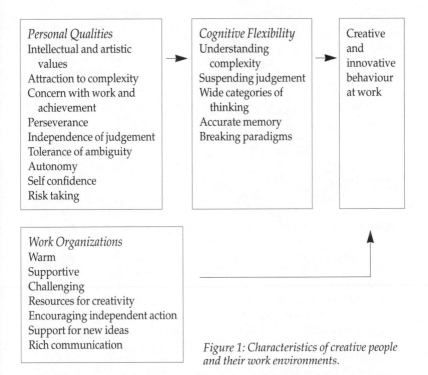

Figure 1: *Characteristics of creative people and their work environments.*

superiors. Clarifying goals and seeking feedback on work performance are also important ways of improving the climate for creativity.

MOTIVATION AND COGNITION

How do creative people derive motivation for the extra effort creativity inevitably demands? Are their thought processes somehow significant? Creative people tend to engage in tasks because of interest, personal challenge or a sense of involvement rather than just engaging in activities to achieve some external goals such as high pay. The thinking and idea-generating processes associated with creativity include flexibility of ideas and flexibility of perceptions of the organizational world. Creative cognitive styles reveal perceptual flexibility, that is, creative people are more prepared to see and experience their worlds in a variety of ways rather than sticking to one tried and tested way. They may see diverse and often competing motives in those around them as well as diverse faces of their organi-

STRENGTHS AND SKILLS

EXERCISE 3

Another way of building confidence in your creativity is to take ten minutes to list your strengths and skills. There is a tendency in some cultures to be modest at the expense of accuracy and you should try to avoid this. Include all those activities at which you are *competent,* not necessarily excellent or perfect. Remember that it is being able to cope in a situation which usually indicates a strength or skill, rather than having total mastery of the situation. Include strengths and skills from all areas of your life – work, home, leisure, child-rearing, gardening, cooking. You may need longer than the ten-minute period, because, as human beings, we have a vast range of strengths and skills which enable us to cope effectively with the myriad of changes which confront us in our lives. Indeed, one of the most fundamental characteristics of being human is our creative ability in many diverse areas. It is useful to add more strengths and skills to your list on a regular basis and to build up a detailed and accurate picture of your own competencies. This picture should never be static since we are constantly learning new skills and discovering new strengths within ourselves.

The value of the list is that it can help to build our confidence. Sometimes in work or non-work situations we face a sudden new major challenge or problem. If we are feeling tired, harassed, incompetent, or small, the problem can seem overwhelming. By reading through our list of strengths and skills we can find new confidence and a sense of competence to overcome the feeling of being unable to cope with the problem or situation. Seeing ourselves in a different and more positive light can be a significant confidence booster and can trigger a surge of creativity in response to the challenges that face us. Moreover, by looking through the list we may see a competence or skill from one area of our lives which usefully transfers across to the area with which we are currently concerned. Some people keep such a list close to hand so that when they are faced with very difficult problems or situations they can derive confidence and strength from reading through the list.

zations. Rather than stereotyping their organizations and their colleagues in a particular way, creative people tend to perceive their work flexibly. They have an ability to think in a variety of ways about the problems which face them at work, and tend to suspend judgement of the nature of problems or of solutions for longer than those who tend to be less creative. This is perhaps a consequence of their tolerance for ambiguity. It means they can suspend judgement, for example about a human relations problem in the workplace where two or more people may be in conflict, until they have gathered a good deal of information and seen the issue from a number of perspectives. They also tend to use wide categories of thinking and to adopt what is sometimes called a 'helicopter' view of problem issues and solutions in the work place – characterized by an ability to take a broad, strategic and wide perspective.

THE INFLUENCE OF THE WORK ENVIRONMENT

Equally important in considering how to stimulate creativity at work is the immediate social and psychological environment of the individual. If the work climate is not supportive of individual creativity, those who derive satisfaction from developing new and improved ways of working will become frustrated and often leave.

Creating a supportive and challenging work environment also promotes confidence in creativity. Research has revealed that warm, supportive and flexible but intellectually demanding environments produce high levels of creativity. Organizations also have to provide appropriate resources for creative efforts and encourage independent action in order to facilitate the creativity of those who work within them. Climates encouraging *interaction, individual autonomy* and *production of new ideas* appear to generate creative achievement in both educational and work organizations. Where climates are characterized by distrust, lack of communication, limited individual autonomy and unclear goals, innovation is more likely to be inhibited.

The work environment described may seem Utopian and remote from the oppressive and restrictive workplaces which many people experience. However, the challenge of this book is to develop creativity and innovation at work; the challenge of being human is not to be restricted by self-imposed perceptions, but to consider how we can develop our own creative characteristics, thinking processes and how we can then change our environments into places where creativity is nurtured rather than stunted.

Measures of the creative climate for individuals in the workplace

MEASURING CREATIVITY

There are many measures of general creativity available, but a number are particularly good.

● The *Torrance Test of Creative Thinking* measures problem-finding as well as creative problem-solving abilities and the validity of this test has been demonstrated in a number of studies.

● Cattell's *16PF*, on the other hand, measures a broad range of personality traits and characterizes the creative person as high in intelligence, dominance, boldness, emotional sensitivity, imagination, radicalism and self sufficiency, but rather low on emotional warmth, impulsivity (that is, more serious) and on diplomacy.

● A widely used measure of creativity in management is the *Kirton Adaptation-Inventory (KAI)* which is described as a measure of creative *style* rather than creative *level*. The questionnaire data reveal two types of people: 'adapters', who tend to be low on originality and high on efficiency and conformity, and 'innovators', who are high on originality and low on efficiency and conformity. Adapters tend to extend existing practices to produce minor innovations whereas innovators tend to change structures rather radically in order to bring about change in their workplaces.

CLIMATE FOR INDIVIDUAL CREATIVITY

EXERCISE 4

Consider the following list and indicate how often your colleagues behave in ways which are supportive. Tick the category which most clearly corresponds to your work experience.

How often do those around you...	Almost never	Very infrequently	Neither frequently nor infrequently	Very frequently	Almost always
Find value in ideas rather than criticize them	☐	☐	☐	☐	☐
Eliminate status	☐	☐	☐	☐	☐
Make boring tasks interesting or challenging	☐	☐	☐	☐	☐
Take relaxation breaks	☐	☐	☐	☐	☐
Give space to creative ideas	☐	☐	☐	☐	☐
Avoid rigour too early on (do not engage in immediate criticism)	☐	☐	☐	☐	☐
Are unrestrained in idea generation	☐	☐	☐	☐	☐
Challenge the rules and go against convention	☐	☐	☐	☐	☐
Challenge organizational constraints	☐	☐	☐	☐	☐
Say 'Yes' to your ideas	☐	☐	☐	☐	☐
Show interest, approval or support for your ideas	☐	☐	☐	☐	☐
Listen to you actively	☐	☐	☐	☐	☐
Look for positive learning in your mistakes	☐	☐	☐	☐	☐
Make challenges fun	☐	☐	☐	☐	☐
Introduce play and humour	☐	☐	☐	☐	☐
Respect the people they work with	☐	☐	☐	☐	☐
Have a positive outlook	☐	☐	☐	☐	☐
Trigger ideas from one another	☐	☐	☐	☐	☐
Encourage an atmosphere of freedom	☐	☐	☐	☐	☐
Draw on your skills	☐	☐	☐	☐	☐
Encourage freedom of discussion	☐	☐	☐	☐	☐
Avoid using ridicule	☐	☐	☐	☐	☐
Reward your creativity	☐	☐	☐	☐	☐

Add up the number of 'Very frequently' or 'Almost always' ticks. Is it more than half the number of questions? If not, consider discussing with your colleagues ways in which together you can better promote a creative climate.

are rare (although good measures of team and organizational climates for creativity and innovation exist (see Chapters 4 and 5). *Exercise 4* shows an example of a measure of climate for individual creativity which can be used to assess the supportiveness of the immediate work environment.

THE NATURE OF THE TASK

The characteristics of the jobs that people do have an impact upon people's ability to be confident in their creativity. Job characteristics are the objective properties of the work that we do, and there are five which appear to be particularly important (Hackman and Oldham, 1980).

1. Skill variety and challenge

Skill variety refers to the degree to which a job requires different activities in order for the work to be carried out and the degree to which the range of skills and talents of the person working within the role is used. Thus, a nurse working with the elderly in their homes may need to use her professional skills of dressing wounds, listening, counselling, being empathic and appraising the supports and dangers in the person's home.

2. Task identity

The concept of task identity refers to the degree to which the job represents a whole piece of work, or to doing a job from beginning to end. It is not simply adding a rubber band to the packaging of a product, but being involved in the manufacture of the product throughout the process, or at least in a meaningful part of the process.

3. Task significance

The importance of the task in terms of its impact upon other people within the organization or in the world at large has an influence on creativity. Monitoring the effectiveness of an organization's debt collection is less significant than applying dressings to the leg ulcers of elderly people in rural settings and may therefore evoke less creativity.

4. Autonomy

This is the degree to which jobs provide freedom, independence and discretion for the people performing them in determining how to do their work and when to it. Their level of autonomy directly determines the extent to which people are creative and innovative in their work.

5. Task feedback

When people receive information about how well they are performing their job and on the effectiveness of their performance, they are more likely to be creative in their work, since they become aware of 'performance gaps'. Consequently, they are more attuned to the need to initiate new ways of working in order to fill the gaps.

If these job characteristics are present, it is more likely that creativity will be manifested in the work, particularly in relation to task autonomy.

Developing individual creativity in the workplace is in part about developing confidence in creativity, and strengthening the personal characteristics associated with creativity. It also requires consideration of how the work environment can be made more supportive of creativity, both in terms of increasing the challenge of work and increasing control over it. But creativity is fundamentally a product of our cognitive processes – how we perceive, think and learn. So how can we develop creative responses?

DEVELOPING CREATIVE RESPONSES TO PROBLEMS

Now we turn to examine ways of increasing cognitive flexibility in practice, by focusing on some simple problems. Following is a series of exercises which encourage creativity in the perspectives we adopt in making decisions and solving problems. Each of these exercises can be solved in many different ways. What they have in common is that they present challenges to how we think about issues in order to find solutions or alternative outcomes.

Each of these problems involves thinking about solutions in radically different ways. Each requires us to free ourselves from limitations, break the rules slightly, see if there are ways that others can help through co-operation and collaboration. Each requires that problems are turned upside down and inside out. Roll them around; consider them from quite different perspectives. Act as if you had come from another world. Compare them with other problems that you encounter every day and see if solutions from other domains can be applied. How would you tell a child to go about solving these problems?

THE CLOCK PUZZLE – TASK AND OBJECTIVES

EXERCISE 5

The task is to tackle a 'puzzle' type problem and to attempt to develop more than one solution. The task demands breaking out of existing ways of looking at things and generating unusual and unexpected solutions to the problem. A further objective is to consider the process of how the problem was tackled, in order to increase your understanding about the nature of creativity and problem-solving. In Diagram 1 there is a clock face which has numerals painted on its glass surface. Imagine that one day the clock falls off the wall and, upon landing, the face breaks into four pieces. Examination of the four pieces reveals that the numerals on each of the pieces add up to give a total which is the same for each of the four pieces. Try to generate explanations for how this might have happened. Remember to be open to your own new ideas for explaining what happened. At the end of the exercise spend some time thinking about how the answers came to you and what the implications are for your own creativity and your methods of finding solutions.

See pp.30–31 for some possible solutions.

NINE DOTS PUZZLE – TASKS AND OBJECTIVES

EXERCISE 6

The task is to tackle the puzzle in Diagram 2 and to develop more than one solution to the problem as presented. Try to break out of existing patterns of solutions and to generate unusual or unexpected solutions to the problem. In Diagram 2 there are nine dots. Your task is to draw no more than four straight lines (without lifting the pencil from the paper), which will cross through all nine dots. Having generated a solution which involves four lines, try to achieve a solution involving only three straight lines. Then try to achieve a two line solution. Finally, try to achieve a one line solution.

See p.31 for some possible solutions.

THE NUN'S JOURNEY

EXERCISE 7

A Buddhist nun set off from the bottom of a mountain exactly at sunrise to walk to the top where there was a glittering temple. A narrow winding path led to the top of the mountain. The nun ascended at varying speeds, stopping along the way to rest and eat dried fruit. She reached the temple before sunset where she stayed for three days fasting and meditating. On the fourth day, she set off back down the mountain, leaving exactly at sunrise. Again, she descended at varying speeds, though her speed going down was faster, on average, than her speed ascending. Prove that there is a spot along the path that the nun occupies on both the ascending and descending journeys at exactly the same time of day.

See p.31 for some possible solutions.

PARADIGMS AND CREATIVITY

As part of the process by which we grow and learn we come to develop frames of reference. These help us make sense of the world and allow us to function in a way which fits in with our particular circumstances and environment. Imagine a fish swimming in a goldfish bowl which never has an awareness of the fact that it is swimming in water because it has never experienced a state of 'out of water'. Its paradigm is different from that of the little girl who sits watching the fish swimming. One way in which we can confront our own paradigms is to try to step outside them and see the world in fresh ways. Practising this can also help to develop our inherent creativity.

As I walk to work each morning passing the trees, bushes and houses in my neighbourhood, I fail to notice the subtle changes in colour consequent upon seasonal change. This is because my paradigm has become a filter preventing me from seeing that which is occurring, in all its beauty and variety. I simply see a relatively unchanging neighbourhood. These paradigms are useful because they prevent us from being overwhelmed by information, but they can also trap us in a perceptual prison which prevents access to wide expanses of creativity.

There are some paradigms of which we are very conscious, such as our political views. But the vast majority are such an integral part of the way in which we think and see that we are often unaware of their existence. They exert a powerful influence over our perceptions, and in particular over our ability to generate new ideas. Sometimes paradigms are so strong that we cannot see what would be obvious to somebody with a different frame of reference, perhaps from a different culture. Visitors to Britain are often more struck by the prevalence of the class system than are people who live in Britain themselves. Not surprisingly the more we have vested in a particular paradigm the harder it is for us to consider alternative perspectives. A visitor from another planet, for example, would perhaps be most struck by the pervasive gender stereotyping and gender classification that occur in work organizations with people restricted to certain status and jobs by their gender, rather than by the nature of the work the organization is conducting.

The more successful we have been in the past, the harder it may be to foresee the paradigm changes of the future. In the 1960s, Switzerland had more than 60 per cent of the world market share in watches, but ten years later its share had fallen to below 10 per cent. The quartz watch has revolutionized the industry and Japanese companies now dominate the market. But ironically, the quartz watch was developed in Switzerland. The then leaders in the Swiss watch making industry were not impressed by the research work on quartz watches, and they assumed that people would not want to buy watches without bearings or gears. The idea was therefore not patented and protected; the new watch did not fit their paradigms. When the researchers displayed the new watch at a conference, two other organizations saw the market potential and developed the idea, thereby innovating successfully and capturing a large part of the watch market.

In considering the three puzzles presented earlier in this chapter, it might be useful to think about what paradigms may prevent people from finding alternative solutions which break rules and how experience of educational institutions, where we are often told that there is only one right answer or one right way (another paradigm of problem-solving), restrict our ability to develop alternative ways of defining problems and generating solutions.

WHEN SHOULD CREATIVITY BE EXERCISED?

A map gives confidence to the traveller moving through unfamiliar territory and having foreknowledge of the route through the creative problem-solving process similarly builds confidence in creativity. Consideration of the stages of creative problem-solving can help people to re-define their understanding of the creative process and to change their paradigms of creative problem-solving. Four well-established stages are:

Stage 1 – Problem exploration
Stage 2 – Generating ideas
Stage 3 – Selecting options
Stage 4 – Implementation

STAGE 1 – PROBLEM EXPLORATION
The most critical stage of problem-solving is the exploration and clarification of the problem. People typically try to develop solutions to problems before clarifying and exploring, and if necessary, re-defining the problems themselves. But the more time spent on exploring and clarifying problems before attempting to seek solutions, the better the quality of the ultimate solutions. Moreover, the

time saved by careful exploration of problems almost always outweighs the time expended on this task. Problem exploration enables us to play with paradigms, reject paradigms, consider new paradigms, and determine whether the problem that we are confronting is simply symptomatic of a deeper problem. Consistent arguing between members of a department may not reflect incompatible personality characteristics, but may be caused by a lack of clarity of departmental goals, or a failure of people to practise the good communication skills of listening to and summarizing each other's positions.

Sometimes people are anxious about identifying the underlying problems within work organizations because this may produce unacceptable threats. Lack of clarity may result from a failure of senior managers to provide clear feedback within the department. Confronting such problems can thus lead to recognition that these are caused by inefficient management or poor communication. Identifying these problems may provoke more anxieties, since it involves criticizing people of higher status, but working to develop solutions to an incorrectly identified problem is obviously inappropriate. Creative problem exploration is thus crucial for the whole process of creative problem-solving and in the next chapter we shall consider in some depth techniques for doing so. These draw on a recognition that problem exploration involves carefully examining and defining the nature of the problem, suspending judgement about the causes of the problem, thinking broadly about what the underlying problem might be, and carefully considering from alternative perspectives how the problem can best be conceptualized.

STAGE 2 – GENERATING IDEAS

Having suspended attempts at solution development during Stage 1, kept response options open as long as possible, suspended judgements and used wide categories, the next step is to develop a range of alternative solutions to the problem. It is characteristic of creative people that they break out of performance scripts, perceive creatively, suspend judgement and generate a variety of solutions to problems. Non-creative people, in contrast, generally seek for one way out – the first minimally acceptable idea is pursued and grasped. However, it is most effective to begin by generating, listing, and then considering in turn a range of possible ways forward. Brainstorming techniques, which involve taking the time to list as many ideas as possible, are best used at this point. It is a stage which should be both playful and challenging, with the aim of generating many new and unrestrained ideas.

STAGE 3 – SELECTING OPTIONS
In this stage it is necessary to be critical and judgmental in thinking about which ideas to develop. In Stage 2 a number of solutions are usually generated, so the three or four solutions which appear most promising should be selected. However, it is important to avoid selecting simply those which fit the existing paradigm. At least one potential solution which involves a completely new way of dealing with the issue should be considered. This stage of critical analysis and selection presents particular difficulties because of a human tendency to select a solution simply because it is a solution rather than because it is the *optimum* solution. Eagerness to achieve closure and to avoid further ambiguity encourages a willingness to overlook problems inherent in adopted solutions. Creative thinking is about keeping response options open as long as possible in order to suspend judgement, break out of performance scripts and perceive creatively.

STAGE 4 – IMPLEMENTATION
If the other three stages have been conducted carefully, implementation is much easier than it would otherwise be, since it a matter of persuading one's colleagues of the usefulness of the solution that has been developed. At the implementation stage, the innovator should gain support in the form of resources, time, and co-operation from managers and others who may influence the effectiveness of the change. Most important when implementing change is to consider the impact of the change upon the various groups or individuals likely to be affected, and to manage the content and process of the change accordingly (see Chapter 6). The most effective way of resolving resistance to change is to involve those likely to resist in the change process. This means interacting with them, sharing information and giving them influence over the decision-making process.

At each of these stages, quite different creative skills are required, and though individuals and groups may not necessarily traverse through them in perfect order, nevertheless, taking time for each is essential for effective decision-making and problem-solving. However, it is critical to ensure that sufficient time has been devoted to carefully exploring and defining the nature of the problem.

Approaching problems or issues at work with a sense of confidence and even pleasure at the prospect of generating a variety of creative ways of exploring or defining the problem, transforms the concept of work itself into an adventure rather than a trial. Having creatively analysed the nature of the problem, we can then creatively develop a range of options or solutions from which to select when dealing with the problem. Even the process of selecting a course of action offers opportunities to deploy the creative strengths all people possess. Finally, there is the process of implementing a selected option within the workplace, which offers opportunities for successfully managing the innovation process within a work setting. This is the most challenging and exciting phase in the innovation process, since it demands that we appreciate and work with the complexities of behaviour in organizations, thereby enriching our understanding of organizational life.

CHAPTER SUMMARY

Individual creativity requires confidence and a supportive and challenging work environment where experimentation and careful risk taking are encouraged. Such creativity can be developed substantially, especially amongst those who have lost confidence in their own creativity. This involves commitment to explore new ideas as well as the determination to believe in personal creativity. But work organizations too can foster this important ability by developing warm, supportive and challenging environments which encourage independent action, provide resources for creativity and facilitate rich communication.

The real voyage of discovery consists not in seeking new landscapes but in having new eyes. Marcel Proust.

PUZZLE SOLUTIONS

Some solutions for the clock puzzle on page 24:

- The clock fell upside-down and was see-through so novel combinations are possible.
- The clock was made of slate and fell into four equal cross sections, with the numbers running through like the lettering on a stick of rock.

- The cracks split between numbers such as the X and I of the number XI.
- The cracks split some numerals such as the X creating two Vs (or fives).
- The number of numerals is counted rather than their value - XII is three numerals rather than the value of twelve.

Some solutions for the nine dots puzzle on page 25:

- Go beyond the boundaries of the puzzle with your lines ● ● ●
- Use a very, very thick pencil (about 3 inches thick!)
- Draw a line around the globe 3 times, traversing through another line of dots on each circumnavigation.
- Cut out the dots and lay them in a single straight line.
- Use a biro with a retractable nib, so that no line is made on the paper as you move from one row of dots to another.

Some solutions to the nun's journey on page 25:

- Imagine two nuns. One leaves the mountain top at sunrise on the same day bound for the bottom of the mountain and following the single path down, as another begins her ascent on the same single path at the same time on the same day. They are bound to meet!
- Draw a graph depicting height on one axis against time of day on the other axis. Then draw in the two journeys (height on the path by time) one beginning from the top of the mountain, the other beginning from the bottom and both at sunrise. Inevitably they intersect. They represent the nun's two journeys, four days apart.
- A spot she occupies on both journeys at the same time of the day is 'the start' of the journey, even thought the start is, in one case the top of the mountain, and in the other, the bottom of the mountain. It may be called, in broad terms, the same spot.

Chapter Three

Becoming an Innovator

We must be the change we wish to see in the world.
Mahatma Gandhi

People frequently change the objectives of their jobs, the methods they use, scheduling, practices, procedures and even whom they deal with and how they deal with them. It is significant that in the job-changing process, people moving into existing jobs are highly innovative and tend to mold and improve the jobs to fit their way of doing things. Moreover, people who have the opportunity to be innovative at work – to introduce new and improved ways of doing things – are far more satisfied with their jobs and better adjusted at work than those who do not have such opportunities. It is remarkable that among managers and professionals whose job moves lead to reduced opportunities to be creative at work, the detriments to their mental health are greater than amongst those managers and professionals who become temporarily unemployed (Nicholson and West, 1988).

Not only is innovation a fundamental part of our behaviour, but the opportunity to be creative and innovative at work is central to our well-being. This is true, not just of managerial and professional workers, but of blue collar workers also. Recent research has indicated that one of the greatest causes of stress at work amongst blue collar assembly line workers is the level of high work demands coupled with the lack of autonomy which inhibits their ability to be creative in and contribute to their work organizations. Most people need to be creative in their work lives, and innovation is a major source of satisfaction at work.

In this chapter, some techniques for developing creativity at work are described. Also explored are techniques that can be used in private to develop your creative ability, including physical relaxation, imaging, dream exploration and 'mindfulness'. For example, *Exercise 5* offers a simple way of becoming aware of the extent of creativity in one's recent work life.

TECHNIQUES FOR PROMOTING CREATIVITY AT WORK

Following are descriptions of some of the techniques which can be used in everyday work settings to develop creative ideas. These techniques are simply aids and are not themselves magical sources of solutions. Creativity is 95 per cent hard work and 5 per cent discovery. When using these techniques, hard effort must be exerted to discover how the ideas generated can help in dealing with work issues or problems. What will not work is a passive approach where the right answers are expected to appear as if by magic, as a result of using the techniques. The techniques are intended to provide new and different ways of looking at issues; wild 'off the wall' alternatives to existing methods of dealing with challenges; and ways of helping to develop new paradigms or new ways of thinking about issues.

Remember:
• creativity involves moulding and sculpting the ideas generated, so that they become appropriate solutions;
• creativity involves working to convert new data into practical ways forward which will enable substantial progress in effective problem-solving.

TECHNIQUE 1: 'TELL ME, STRANGER ...'

This technique is particularly suited for the problem clarification and exploration stage of the decision-making process. On the basis that those closest to a situation will sometimes have difficulty in stepping back and seeing it clearly, the exercise involves talking to someone outside the situation to help make progress in decision-making. It involves identifying a 'stranger' and explaining to them the nature of the problem or decision which we are facing, their function being to help us explore and clarify the problem. They ask questions for further information and clarification, and seek initially not to offer any solutions or ideas for ways forward. It is particularly valuable to choose somebody whose functional area is very dissimilar. In this

INNOVATION LOG

EXERCISE 8

List all of the innovations you remember introducing into your work in the last year. Remember that innovation does not mean making a major technological or administrative change. It is any new and improved way of doing things which you have intro- duced which may have affected your job or the jobs of those you supervise or work with. It may have affected your customers, service receivers, colleagues or team. Consider how satisfying it was to have effectively implemented the inno- vation and what successes, difficulties and resistances you encountered on the way. This will give you some insight into the fact that innovation is often associated with conflict and resistance, but also can be a source of satisfaction in repre- senting the fruition of your creative activities.

Innovations I introduced at work within the last year:

1. . . . .

Successes . . . .

Difficulties . . . .

Resistance . . . .

2. . . . .

Successes . . . .

Difficulties . . . .

Resistance . . . .

3. . . . .

Successes . . . .

Difficulties . . . .

Resistance . . . .

way we are required to explain the problem more carefully and more clearly. The process of explaining a problem to someone who is not familiar with the domain can lead to new understanding about appropriate ways forward. By having to verbalize, clarify and systematize presentation of the problem, the nature of the problem often becomes much clearer. Indeed, personal counselling is defined as the process of exploring and clarifying a problem; it is not necessarily about finding solutions. Moreover, the stranger may ask 'naïve' questions which lead us to re-assess our basic assumptions. Finally, simply taking time to discuss the problem with another person in itself can be very helpful.

An appropriate strategy in organizations is for people to take 20 minutes each to explore their problem. Person A presents his or her problem, while person B acts as the stranger/counsellor for 20 minutes. Then person B presents his or her problem while person A takes the role of counsellor. Each person has equal time to explore and clarify their particular situation.

The second stage of the problem is asking the 'stranger' to come up with a particular idea or way forward. Within the last five minutes of the exercise the counsellor is invited to offer one particular solution or way forward. The onus however, is on the person who 'owns' the problem to build on that suggestion. The counsellor's opinion, no matter how bizarre, is examined to see whether elements of the opinion can be used to generate new and useful ideas. The exercise also assumes that a stranger to the situation may have a different mental 'paradigm' which may be useful in generating creative alternatives. This is not a revolutionary technique. Many of us use the 'tell me, stranger' technique when we get home from work and talk over particular situations with partners or friends. Sometimes, this is not possible because of time constraints or because of a concern not to bring work problems back to the home. One strategy, therefore, is to find a 'stranger' (someone not familiar with your work area, but whom you can trust) within your organization and arrange to meet on a regular or when the need arises basis to help clarify problems or generate solutions. This can also be done over the telephone, but relaxed face-to-face meetings are generally more effective. One meeting a month need take no more than an hour or two of people's time, and it is a good use of that time. Having lunch together may make the process even more convivial. There is much research evidence which indicates that when people take time out to review and clarify problems carefully, they are strategically much more effective in the long run.

TECHNIQUE 2: TRANSPORTING CREATIVE ENERGY TO WORK

This exercise enables people to respond to challenge and change with extra energy and creativity by drawing upon knowledge of what motivates them in their lives, and looking for ways to bring the qualities of that motivation to work activities. The exercise can be done either alone or, better, in pairs. If done in pairs, one person takes the role of client and the other the role of counsellor. The counsellor asks a series of straightforward questions and notes down the answers given by the client. These are then available for the client to reflect upon. Each person takes about 20 minutes to act as a client and then swops roles and acts as counsellor. The session involves the counsellor asking the clients four sets of questions:

1. *What activity, in any area of your life, do you really enjoy? What activity makes you feel as though you are 'in flow', complete, at one, really in touch with yourself or very effective in the world? What activity do you really enjoy?*

2. *What makes that activity so special for you? Why do you get so much enjoyment out of it? What is the essence of that activity for you?*

3. *How could you bring the qualities of that activity into your work life to enable you to be more creative and effective? How could you alter some of your work activities so that the qualities of the enjoyable activity are brought into your work life?*

4. *What lessons are there in this for understanding about your creativity and energy at work?*

Example
Counsellor
What activity in your life gives you enormous enjoyment?

Client
I really enjoy running in wild, empty, open and natural places like the hills or along the cliffs.

Counsellor
What makes that activity so special for you?

Client
I enjoy the sense of freedom and being dependent just on me. I also feel more relaxed in a natural environment – the sense of fresh air and well-being.

Counsellor

How could you bring some of those qualities to your work, such as freedom, well-being, independence and naturalness of the environment?

Client

That's difficult, but I could try and do more projects on my own so I wouldn't be dependent on others for all of them. I could do a lot to make my office a more pleasant environment by putting in some pictures and plants. I think I could also take time out to relax more in the office, rather than just driving myself without taking time to stop and appreciate what I have achieved. I tend to do that in running, but I don't do it in my work. I could also take time out now and again to go for a short walk to get some fresh air and make some contact with the natural environment, like the park just down the road from the office.

Counsellor

What lessons does this hold for your creativity and energy at work more generally?

Client

Well, I do get really caught up in the routine of work and don't think about what might give me more energy or what might make work more exciting and enjoyable. I have just realized, as well, that one of the things I like about running is the challenge of how far I am going to go or whether I am going to make some of the big hills in the run. At work too I can rethink some of the things I see as big problems into big challenges and long distances. If I set myself targets and see them as challenges rather than threats, then that would make me more effective, energetic and creative at work.

This example illustrates how the exercise can reveal new perspectives on work and on what is important in our lives. It is a technique which can help change the humdrum experience of some of our work into excitement and creativity. It involves pushing back boundaries and drawing upon deeper experience of what is important to us and transferring that to the world of work.

TECHNIQUE 3: RANDOM INPUT

Another method of breaking out of paradigms, habitual ways of thinking or mind sets is to generate random input in our thinking systems. A simple way of doing this is to use a dictionary. Identify an area of work where you would like to generate some new ideas in helping you to find solutions. Write down a clear statement of the issue. Open a dictionary at random and again, at random, put your finger on any word. Then consider whether the word throws up any association of ideas which might be even vaguely relevant to the area of work you are considering. Write down the random word you have chosen and any ideas which come up in association with it. This may point you towards new ways of thinking about the situation. This exercise should be fun and should stimulate creativity, but an effort must be made to use the input to find new ideas. Creativity is 5 per cent 'Eureka!' and 95 per cent hard work.

Example - How to be more effective in selecting candidates for jobs
Random word: 'YOU'
Idea generated
Have the candidate interview you about the job and your managerial practices and about the organization. This may give you more information about the candidate's thinking about selection in organizations and about his or her interests in the work than if the interview is conducted the other way around.

Random word: 'THIGH'
Idea generated
Ask candidates about their interests in sport since there is some association between high levels of stress of work and lack of physical fitness. There is also some evidence that people who are physically fit tend to perform better at work.

Random word: 'BRISTLING'
Idea generated
Ask interviewees to indicate how they would characteristically handle difficult or aggressive people, to give an idea of how they would cope with social interaction at work.

Random word: 'OBSERVATION'
Idea generated
Give the candidates some task to perform in a group and use assessment centre type techniques to observe their performance in those social and task-centred situations.

Each of the three techniques described emphasizes a different, but important, element in creativity and innovation processes at work.

The first focuses on the value of changing paradigms and discovering fresh perspectives. The second demonstrates the need to bring energy to creativity and innovation at work, and the third draws attention to the use of images, metaphors or analogies in thinking about innovation at work. Indeed, research with creative people indicates that they tend to use metaphors and images in their thinking and speech much more than others.

Like any other skill that we deploy at work it is necessary to commit time for practice; to develop strategies for discovering creative ideas; and to put effort and energy into developing creative processes. A three-day training course once every four or five years is unlikely to significantly develop creativity. To nourish creative potential and reap the value requires giving time to develop action plans for encouraging creativity and innovation, and time to think through work-related issues or problems in creative ways. That being so, we shall now turn to explore a very different and fundamentally important orientation to creative problem-solving.

LETTING CREATIVE SOLUTIONS FIND YOU

A growing problem in the world of work is the increasing demands on reduced numbers of people. Performance management systems, 'stretch objectives' and 'leaner organizations', all demand more of employees. Attempts to manage organizational cultures often have the aim of raising the commitment of people in organizations to a level which may be unhealthy. The resulting stress is comparable to the consequences of driving a car in first gear at high speed over a long period of time. Human beings are not designed to be driven flat out full-time. We need time for rest, nourishment, rejuvenation, recuperation, refreshment and stillness. We need the peace from which much creativity can burst.

In many educational establishments and work organizations the focus of activity is largely on improving productivity and performance using convergent thinking and a belief in correct solutions. It is not surprising that so many of us approach problem-solving in an active, solution-seeking way. The typical orientation towards finding creative solutions is characterized by striving, concentration, focus, hard work and a kind of internalized drive towards coming up with correct answers or creative solutions. The kinds of words which can be used to describe this approach are: *active, urgent, energetic, production-oriented, striving, determined, dogged, persistent* and *closed focus.*

However, there is an entirely different approach to the discovery of creative solutions which involves *letting go*. It is a still, relaxed, intuitive approach to finding problems, solutions and creative options and is less frequently used or understood in work organizations. This approach assumes that our inherent creative capacities are rich and available to us at all times, irrespective of whether we are consciously aware of the solutions we are trying to find. In this approach to creativity, people sense solutions via intuition, or by allowing images to arise, being relaxed, or drawing on experiences such as dream images, or through practising techniques such as meditation. Words which describe this approach include *intuition, acceptance, stillness, calm, meditation, openness, mindfulness, the unconscious, passive alertness, open focus, spontaneous, fun, playfulness, in-flow*. Following are descriptions of some techniques for the development of this accepting orientation to the development of creative responses.

PHYSICAL RELAXATION

Research evidence has shown that people's arousal levels in work or in other settings can rise very quickly when they feel threatened, angry or afraid, but the return to base line takes longer. Stress at work can lead to people feeling pressured and unsafe, and in such conditions people's creative abilities are suppressed. The regular practice of relaxation exercises can both ameliorate the effects of stressful environments and also can enable people to more fully develop their creative potential. (See *Exercise 9*.)

USING IMAGES

Metaphors and images can be used to generate different perspectives at work. One way of developing creativity is to practise using language in a creative way. Creative metaphors are different from the clichés of everyday speech which require no work or creativity from us (for example, 'as quick as a flash'; 'as hard as nails'; 'he is a beast of a man'). We can learn to develop the use of original metaphors and images in our speech which ensure that we become more creative in thinking and everyday use of language. For example, 'The walk home through the park to work every day is as refreshing as a mountain waterfall. Then I arrive home to a shower of children's voices and a rushing stream of bodies'; 'Dealing with 'the pinball ricochets' of relationships of people at work can be tiresome'; 'I'm completing

PHYSICAL RELAXATION

EXERCISE 9

To practise physical relaxation, find a quiet location where you are not likely to be disturbed and give yourself a space of 10 to 20 minutes in which to enjoy the process of relaxation. This exercise can be done lying down or sitting, whichever is most comfortable.

Sit quietly for a minute or so with your eyes closed and just allow yourself to relax into a sense of stillness. Then let your attention go to your feet and ankles and allow your feet and ankles to relax, letting go of any tightness or tension. An important principle to remember in this exercise is that there is no need to try to achieve any particular level of relaxation. The relaxation response is a natural response. If you <u>try</u> to relax, you do the opposite of what is intended. The real skill in this exercise is <u>learning not to try</u>, learning to <u>let go</u>. We are all used to trying hard to do things right the first time but in this type of exercise there is no trying or forcing, you simply let it happen.

Then take your attention to your calf muscles and again, just by letting your attention dwell there, let go of any tightness or tension. Let the muscles relax. Continue in this way, turning your attention to various areas of your body and allowing each to relax in turn:

Knees, Thighs, Pelvic area, Lower part of the back, Middle of the back, Upper part of the back, Stomach/chest area, Fingers, Palms of the hands, Wrists, Forearms, Elbows, Upper arms, Shoulders, Jaw area, Mouth, Lips, Neck, Face including the cheeks and the nose, Eyes, Forehead, Rest of your head.

So by taking your attention to the different parts of the body and, just for a short time, letting your attention dwell there, you allow the tightness and tension to drain away. Finally, take three deep breaths and on each out-breath, breathe out very fully, allowing yourself to relax even more deeply. Then you should sit quietly for three or four minutes, just enjoying the quietness and stillness and warmth associated with this deep relaxation. When you are ready, move gently in your chair and take a long slow stretch, slowly bringing your body back into activity and movement. Then when you are ready, very slowly open your eyes, bit by bit as though you were watching the dawn creeping in.

This exercise can be practised once or twice a day. With time it becomes much easier to allow relaxation to occur. The trick is in letting the relaxation happen, rather than trying to achieve a particular level of relaxation.

tasks all day long as though I was batting away an onslaught of tennis balls'. Practising original use of images in speech and writing develops our own creative thinking as well as that of those around us; rich use of language demands cognitive flexibility from both the speaker and listener.

However, rather than simply using metaphors in speech or using analogies to generate new ideas, it is also possible to use exercises which enhance imagery processes. Here the aim is to allow images to appear as you relax and let go and to see whether these images can be used to give insights into the particular problem or issue you are facing. Of course when one adopts a relatively passive approach to generating images, the particular symbols or images which occur may not represent input to the creative problem which you begin with. It could be another major issue in your life or in your work experience to which these images apply. The point of passive, intuitive approaches is that they are not goal-directed and there may be some deeper issue which you are currently facing to which these images speak. Try *Exercise 10*.

The value of imagery is often exemplified by the story of F. A. Kekulé von Stradonitz who discovered the structure of the benzene molecule and thereby built the table of chemical elements. Having struggled to understand the structure of the benzene molecule, he played with images of snakes chasing each other, one night as he sat before the fire. He eventually imagined the snakes chasing and then biting their own tails and thus stumbled upon the notion that the benzene molecule was a closed structure. He immediately wrote down this possible solution and from that the answer to the problem emerged.

THE IMAGERY OF DREAMS

Managers and professionals in major corporations are remarkably open to exploring normal ways of developing their creativity, probably because they attach great importance to innovations in the workforce. Indeed, one technique I have used in major corporations such as British Petroleum and IBM is encouraging professionals to explore their unconscious and the content of dreams. For example, they are asked to discover, through their dreams, the meaning behind the following string of letters:

HIJKLMNO

They are asked to consider such problems carefully before they sleep.

CREATIVE IMAGERY

EXERCISE 10

Again, give yourself a space of 20 minutes or so to relax and practise the use of imaging for developing creative solutions.

● Sit or lie down with your eyes closed.

● Imagine you are in a very pleasant, safe meadow on a warm summer's day.

● Prepare to set off on a journey to a mountain in the distance.

● Set off on the journey enjoying the sights of trees, flowers and animals along the way.

● After a period of time you come upon a dwelling place.

● Examine the dwelling place carefully – what sort of place is it?

● Enter the dwelling and take a few minutes to notice what kind of place it is inside and notice objects, people or animals.

● Having explored the dwelling carefully, set out on the journey again towards the mountain.

● When you arrive at the base of the mountain you will find an object. Examine this object carefully – what does it say to you? What does it mean for you? Take some time to study it.

● Decide whether to leave the object where you found it or to take it with you on your journey to the top of the mountain.

● Set off again.

● When you come to the middle of the mountain there will be another object. Locate this object and examine it carefully. Again, take a few minutes to do this.

● Decide whether to take the object with you up the mountain or to leave it where it is.

● Set off up the mountain again.

● When you reach the top of the mountain you will find a third object. Again, take a few minutes to examine the object carefully. Consider what it says to you and what it means for you.

continued

continued _

● Enjoy the view around the mountain and the vistas that you can see from the top.

● Next, you meet a wise person who perhaps has a message for you in relation to the issue you are currently facing.

● Greet the person and listen carefully to the message if there is one.

● Say goodbye to the wise person and prepare to return to the meadow.

● Start your journey back to the meadow.

● The journey is much easier and you feel more refreshed with every step along the way.

● Arrive back at the meadow and enjoy the sense of peace and rest and refreshment which you have.

● When you are ready, very gently open your eyes, bit by tiny bit, as though you were watching the dawn creeping in.

Now consider carefully the images and symbols that were evoked in this imaginary journey. What clues might some of these images give you for creative ideas or creative solutions to the problems that you are facing? Remember to put effort into thinking how these images may have value for you. Write down the details of your journey (or draw a picture) and see if, in thinking through those details both after the exercises and subsequently, there are useful clues for creative solutions or ways forward.

MOZART: A CASE STUDY IN CREATIVITY

Information from any area of life can inform creative solutions in other areas. One of Mozart's passions was billiards. While playing the game he watched and listened to the changing rhythms and patterns of sound associated with the billiard balls hitting the table cushions and hitting other billiard balls. From this he generated new ideas for his musical creations.

The following morning they are asked to discover if their dreams gave them clues. In many cases, these managers and professionals are able to solve particular problems using their dream imagery. The solution to the problem in the example is H_2O (H to O!) or water, and many participants in our workshops report dreams which are rich in water images and some make the connection between these images and the puzzle, spontaneously finding the solution.

In order to remember dreams it is helpful to rehearse your intention just before sleep by repeating, 'I will remember my dreams. I will remember my dreams. I will remember my dreams'. Keep a notepad and pencil by the side of your bed so that when you wake you can jot down the details of your dreams. Very often when we wake from dreams we are convinced that we will be able to remember them the following day, but a further period of sleep seems to erase our memories. Having a notebook by the side of the bed is a useful way of encouraging yourself to record dream images. After repeating the process three or four nights running, people are virtually guaranteed to remember in detail the content of dreams. Such dream content is valued in many cultures but has been neglected in Western industrial cultures where the importance of unconscious approaches to problem-solving has been downplayed. Dream images *can* be used to uncover hidden answers to puzzling problems.

MEDITATION

Meditation is a method of increasing relaxation and encouraging awareness of the world which is widely practised in many cultures. Its value in encouraging creativity has also been suggested by some research studies. Indeed, many researchers argue for the importance of 'mindfulness' in work in order to increase awareness of the broader problems, rather than losing direction in a torrent of detail.

What is meditation?

One day a man of the people said to Zen master Ikkyu, 'Master, will you please write for me some maxims of the highest wisdom?'

Ikkyu immediately took his brush and wrote the word 'Attention'.

'Is that all?' asked the man. 'Will you not add something more?'

Ikkyu then wrote twice running: 'Attention. Attention.'

'Well,' remarked the man rather irritably, 'I really don't see much depth or subtlety in what you have just written'.

Then Ikkyu wrote the same word three times running: 'Attention. Attention. Attention.'

Half-angered, the man demanded, 'What does that word "Attention" mean anyway?'

And Ikkyu answered gently, 'Attention means attention'. (Kapleau, 1980.)

Essentially, the Zen master explained what meditation is – simply learning to pay attention. The breathing exercise described in *Exercise 11* is a simple introduction to meditation practice. Approached with an open, contented frame of mind and heart, meditation practice can help to increase receptivity, awareness and openness to the rich images and experience which enable creative discovery and expression.

MINDFULNESS

One of the problems with being trapped by paradigms and sucked into the whirlpool urgency of the world of work is that we are often unaware of the myriad of factors which may be influencing our behaviour and that of others at work. Mindfulness techniques involve *a simple quiet awareness of all that is here and now* and can be practised by the modern manager as he or she wanders through his or her working life. Mindfulness involves being mindful of other people, work circumstances, one's own sensations and feelings, the nature of the work environment, the overall objective. An open, accepting but disciplined mindfulness – the commitment to maintaining awareness of all that is here and now in one's experiences at work – can lead to a deepening of intuition and a much wider approach to the problems of the workplace. We are less likely to get sucked into strengthening the defence mechanisms that organizations use (ways of avoiding coping with the real problems of the workplace) and inappropriate paradigms. Practising mindfulness in meetings is a valuable way of becoming aware of not just the content of discussions in meetings, but the processes which underlie them. Are people competing for power and status in meetings as well as talking about work-related issues? Are people talking for the sake of having their voices heard rather than because they wish to contribute valuable and useful ideas? Is one's own participation in the meeting a useful constructive participation? This present-centred awareness of work is a valuable wellspring for creativity. It is characterized by attentiveness, connection, integration (physically, intellectually and emotionally) and focus; 'Presence is manifested by the person's aliveness to and in particular situations' (Kahn, 1992).

A SIMPLE MEDITATION

EXERCISE 11

Close your eyes.

Enjoy the stillness and quietness of sitting silently for a moment and let your attention go to your breath.

Just mentally watch your breathing. You may be 'watching' your stomach as it moves with your breathing; or your chest when it rises and falls; the sensation of breathing in your throat; the sensation of breath in your nostrils; or the sensation of your breathing at the point when the breath enters and leaves your nostrils. It doesn't matter where – just wherever feels comfortable.

Allow your attention to dwell on your breathing and each time you breathe out say the word 'one' silently to yourself.

It is not necessary to concentrate on your breathing and saying the word 'one' at all times. From time to time you may drift away on a train of thought or a noise may distract you. When you become aware that you have drifted away, very gently come back to watching your breath and repeating the word 'one'. As easily as you moved away from the focus on breathing and repeating the word 'one', move back again to this focus, very gently and easily. Remember to take it easy, quietly and gently at all times.

In dealing with intrusive thoughts or sounds, remember to adopt a very open, contented attitude. Treat such thoughts as you would treat clouds drifting across the sky. You don't push them away and you don't hold on to them. Just watch them come and go. Then when you feel ready, go back very easily to watching the breath and repeating the word 'one'.

This open, contented, accepting awareness of breathing is a fundamental orientation to the meditative process. The focus on breathing supplies a valuable but gentle discipline to the meditation exercise. This breathing meditation practice is widely practised in cultures throughout the world. By practising a meditation technique such as this on a daily basis for 10 minutes once or twice a day there can be an increase in relaxation and possible increases in creativity as a consequence.

CHAPTER SUMMARY

In this chapter techniques for developing creativity have been described. Some focus upon putting effort into the creative process by using input from diverse areas, using analogies and giving sufficient time and energy to clarifying problems. The notion of 'letting go' of problems or issues in order that intuitive and deeper creative processes have an opportunity to manifest was also described. However, in order to implement innovation effectively in the world of work it is clear that the individual innovator is a lone revolutionary. One person revolutionary parties rarely succeed. However, small groups committed to a vision can have a powerful impact in bringing about change. In the next chapter we shall consider team innovation and how creating a small committed team can lead to such revolutionary changes in organizations. Before moving on, try assessing your innovativeness at work by completing *Exercise 12*.

Keep a 'don't know' mind. Only keep a 'don't know' mind.
Zen proverb

HOW INNOVATIVE ARE YOU AT WORK?

EXERCISE 12

The following questionnaire explores your feelings about innovation and change at work. How far do you agree or disagree with the following statements?

	Strongly disagree 1	Disagree 2	Not sure 3	Agree 4	Strongly agree 5
I try to introduce improved methods of doing things at work.	☐	☐	☐	☐	☐
I have ideas which significantly improve the way the job is done.	☐	☐	☐	☐	☐
I suggest new working methods to the people I work with.	☐	☐	☐	☐	☐
I contribute to changes in the way my team works.	☐	☐	☐	☐	☐
I am receptive to new ideas which I can use to improve things at work.	☐	☐	☐	☐	☐

Now add up your score. The average score for 250 employed males and females on this scale was 19.0. If you score 20 or over, you have a high propensity to innovate. If your score is high, it is more likely you will produce and implement creative ideas.

(Burningham and West, 1995)

Chapter Four

Creative Teams at Work

The very essence of leadership is that you have to have vision. You can't blow an uncertain trumpet.
Theodore Hesburgh

In response to complexity and change, many organizations have made the team the functional unit of the organization. Instead of individuals being responsible for separate pieces of work, groups of individuals come together to combine their efforts, knowledge and skills to achieve shared goals. Consequently, for *organizations* to be innovative, *teams* must also be innovative, adaptable and essentially creative in their response to problems within the organization and in the wider environment. In this chapter, the fundamental factors influencing team creativity are described, and techniques for promoting team creativity are outlined.

Human ingenuity in a value-free context expresses itself in myriad ways that can be constructive, destructive, political, acquisitive, abusive, or nurturing. In organizational settings we have examples of how human ingenuity has been used to develop means of mass destruction; ways of exploiting others; ways of addicting people so that they squander their resources unwisely; and methods of deceit that attack fundamental principles of human relationships. Organizations are not necessarily benign agents in which we should unthinkingly foster ingenuity or creativity. Ingenuity in a value-free context can be as much a threat as a benefit to society.

Team creativity from this point of view involves the shared development and application of ideas that help society in adaptive ways. Whereas ingenuity can be merely an arid search for novel combinations of disparate conceptual elements, team creativity has a deeper reality – the discovery of meaning through new ways of seeing patterns in the world. Innovation is then the application of that team creativity in ways that are beneficial in society.

As organizations become increasingly complex in response to environments that grow ever more changeable in their social, political, and economic character, the actions of individuals within organizations become decreasingly influential. Individuals rarely bring about change within organizations; teams more often do. Teams have the resilience, range of skills, abilities, and experience to ensure that creative ideas are put into innovative practice. Societal changes, too, are often initiated through the activities of small groups of committed, persistent individuals whose values may well lie outside the acceptable social range. What factors determine whether a team is likely to be effective in bringing about creative change? Much of what follows is based on research evidence I and my colleagues have gathered from teams in a wide variety of organizational settings (West, 1994).

TEAM VISIONS

For a team to be creative it must have vision to give focus and direction to creative energies. This is not some empty mission statement espousing motherhood and apple pie and hiding a poverty of orientation in action. Vision for a team should be a clear, shared, negotiated, attainable, and evolving ideal of some valued future outcome. To a primary health care team it might be enabling patients to take responsibility for their health by giving them a sense of power and control over their own physical health outcomes. There are a number of dimensions along which the vision of a team can be understood.

VISION CLARITY
Many teams do not take time to explore and articulate their objectives and attempt to encapsulate these into a vision statement. In other cases the vision may be quite appropriately implicit rather than explicit. Motivating implicit visions influences creativity far more than explicit but artificially fashioned mission statements.

SHARED VISION
If team members do not share a team vision, their individual creativity cannot be pooled to produce creative team outcomes. This

implies that visions are also negotiated, because members of teams do not come together with identical values and visions. When the team leader or organizational hierarchy determines rather than influences the 'vision' for a team, the vision is unlikely to be shared and will have little influence upon creativity. Where there is a strong shared sense of valued goals or orientations within a team, it is much more likely that commitment and creativity will be engendered and employed. Visions must therefore be negotiated by team members coming together, working through their differences to find a consensual sense of their valued orientation.

EVOLVING VISIONS

The foregoing necessarily implies that a vision should be evolving. Visions are reflections of human values, interests, expectancies, and beliefs. Because people develop and change and because teams develop and change, the vision itself must evolve over time. A vision that is not reviewed and modified as part of team development becomes merely a marker of their past.

TEAM PARTICIPATION

All this requires that teams be participative. Participation is a means to reduce resistance to change, encourage commitment, and produce a more human-oriented 'culture'. It incorporates three fundamental concepts: *influence over decision-making, information sharing,* and *interaction.*

INFLUENCE OVER DECISION-MAKING

Where team members have influence over decision-making, they are more likely to contribute their creative ideas. Indeed, all team members should take responsibility for aspects of team functioning, rather than assuming that the team leader is responsible for objectives, strategies, and processes. There are times, however, when it is inappropriate for all members to make a decision. True team participation occurs when the processes of decision-making are collectively determined, but where particular decisions are placed in the hands of individuals. Decision-making in this way does not become a paralysis of action. It is not a process of empty consultation designed to placate the members of the group. Such participation ensures that the views, experience, and abilities of all within the team are added to the pallet of ideas with which the team will paint the future.

INFORMATION SHARING

Unless people within teams communicate and share information in an open-hearted and generous way, the team can miss the opportunities to generate creative new ways of doing things. But information sharing, too, holds its disadvantages if team members simply overwhelm one another with e-mail messages or written memoranda. Richness of information is determined by the medium through which the information is channelled. E-mail messages and written memoranda are impoverished media for information sharing; the richest form of information sharing is face-to-face communication. Thus, teams should encourage face-to-face communication and use written media only for simple messages.

INTERACTION FREQUENCY

Frequency of interaction of team members will necessarily determine the extent to which they exchange ideas, information, and conflicting views, and will therefore enrich their collective bank of knowledge and creative opportunities. When team members avoid one another to avoid conflict, they are essentially avoiding opportunities for creativity and creative consensus.

SAFETY

Creativity is about things new and different: the untried and untested; things that may fail; things that may generate resistance and conflict. Creativity is about taking risks. Team members are only willing to try out new ideas, and to risk appearing foolish, if they feel safe from ridicule or attack. In so many areas of human behaviour the same phenomenon is found. The client who feels a sense of safety, warmth, and empathy from the psychotherapist is more likely to risk giving voice to denied or repressed experiences. Similarly, we are likely to play with new and different ideas to the extent that we find that our team provides a sense of safety and support in the expression of those ideas.

TASK ORIENTATION

High task orientation, which is critically necessary to team creativity, is characterized by *reflexivity, constructive controversy, tolerance of minority ideas,* and *commitment to excellence.*

REFLEXIVITY

Reflexivity is fundamentally important in ensuring the appropriateness of team strategies and processes and task outcomes. The more that teams take time to reflect critically upon their objectives, strategies, and processes, and then, crucially, modify them, the more creative and effective are they likely to be. Many teams argue that they are too overwhelmed by demands to take time for such reflection, yet there is abundant evidence that doing so leads to more effective and creative outcomes. Such reflexivity, however, carries with it risks that *more* uncertainty rather than *less* may be created, that existing processes and strategies of the team may be challenged, that new ones may have to be sought. Yet, it is the ability to live with uncertainty and ambiguity and readily adapt in the face of changing demands, while sticking firmly to the evolving vision, that characterizes creative, effective teams.

CONSTRUCTIVE CONTROVERSY

In the teams that practise these principles, there is a high level of 'constructive controversy' where team members feel their competence is affirmed rather than attacked, where there is a climate of co-operation and trust rather than a climate of competition and distrust, and where critical review is seen as a constructive process rather than a destructive, aggressive conflict. In such teams there is a concern with excellence of outcomes and not with the individualistic ambitions of team members.

MINORITY INFLUENCE

The extent to which a team can tolerate within its membership a minority who adopt differing views is an important determinant of creativity. Much, if not all, creativity is applied in practice via conflict; that is, by overcoming resistance to change in others. The team itself may be a minority within an organization, not just encouraging new and improved ways of doing things, but, by its stands, encouraging independent and creative thinking and acting more widely within the organization. Minorities influence others through processes of conversion and conflict, which enable other minorities to express their differing creative views. All of which is of great importance in organizations that seek to adapt to the ever-changing and increasingly complex world we are creating. How a team manages a minority within its membership is an important indicator of its ability to be a creative adaptive social unit.

SUPPORT FOR INNOVATION

I and my colleagues have repeatedly found that support for innovation emerges as the most significant predictor of the innovation and creativity of teams. But support has two distinct elements: *espoused* support and *active* support. In many teams support for innovation is espoused, but when the practicalities of support are examined, it is rare for team members or top management to give time, resources, and co-operation for the development of new ideas. Yet it is precisely these activities that determine the extent to which creativity within teams occurs. If new ideas are accepted and encouraged verbally, but team members do not provide the necessary practical support, the platitudes of verbal encouragement soon lose their currency.

Creativity in organizations is associated with uncertainty, ambiguity, conflict, and risk. The ideas offered here are not some easy remedy for teamwork, without danger or difficulty. Developing a negotiated, shared, and evolving vision means accepting uncertainty over time and encouraging, not minimizing, change. It also involves giving up some control to enable team members to develop their own vision, which may well be at variance with that of other teams in the organization. This is the stuff of creativity. There are risks and opportunities in participation, with team members taking, rather than avoiding, responsibility for decision-making and maximizing rich means of communication. Such participation enables the group to become a vital, evolving social unit, the creative energies of which are released, but with unpredictable outcomes. Reflexivity involves challenge to existing ways of doing things. This may mean encouraging uncertainty in the face of rapid change, rather than attempting to minimize it, which is often our natural reaction. But our world is changing by our own making, and old ways of responding to changing circumstances are no longer helpful.

Thus far we have considered some of the major group processes characterizing creative teams. Next we described a variety of factors in the organizational context and in the composition of teams which impact upon their creativity. These influencing factors in relation to team innovation are depicted in *Figure 2*.

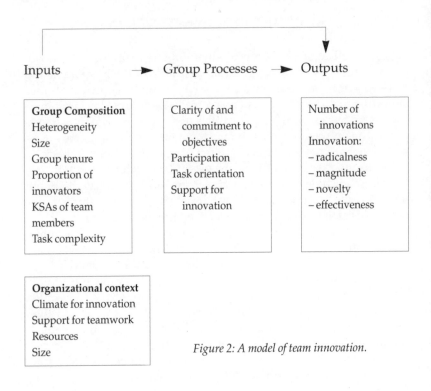

Figure 2: A model of team innovation.

TEAM COMPOSITION

Research on the relationship between team size and creativity shows that larger teams tend to be less creative. This may be simply because as teams grow the effectiveness of communication processes is diminished and problems of co-ordination are increased. In general the maximum team size for relatively high levels of creativity is between ten and twelve people. Teams are most effective when they have sufficient, but not greater than sufficient, numbers of members to perform the group task. Very small teams (two or three people) may lack the diversity of view points and perspectives necessary for innovation, while large teams (above twelve or thirteen) may become too unwieldy to enable effective interaction, exchange and participation. There is also strong evidence that for creative decision-making tasks, team diversity (in terms of personality, training, background and gender) is of importance for high quality team decision-making.

HOW INNOVATIVE IS YOUR TEAM AT WORK?

EXERCISE 13

Compared with other similar teams, how innovative do you consider your team to be?
Circle the appropriate response for the following task areas.

	Highly stable: few changes introduced		Moderately innovative: some changes introduced		Highly innovative: many changes introduced
Setting work targets or objectives	1	2	3	4	5
Deciding the methods used to achieve objectives/targets	1	2	3	4	5
Initiating new procedures or information systems	1	2	3	4	5
Developing innovative ways of accomplishing targets/objectives	1	2	3	4	5
Initiating changes in the job contents and work methods of your staff	1	2	3	4	5

Total score ☐

Low Score	=	5 to 13
Average Score	=	14 to 18
High Score	=	19 to 25

This may stem in part from the diversity of perspectives team members can bring to the decision-making process.

LIFE TIME OF THE TEAM

There are creativity differences consequent upon the team's tenure. Longer tenure is associated with increasing team homogeneity and consequent deleterious effects on team innovation. Longer serving teams can become complacent about being alert for changes in the organization and their wider environment. Groups that have been together for a long period may tend to ignore and become increasingly isolated from others within and outside the organization, especially those that provide the most critical feedback, evaluation and information. Without changes in membership too, groups may become less innovative over time. Project newcomers can enhance creativity within teams since they challenge and often broaden existing practices.

CHARACTERISTICS OF TEAM MEMBERS

Another element of group composition is the personality of group members. Recent research has suggested that team innovation will be affected partly by the proportion of creative and innovative individuals who constitute the team. The generation of new ideas within a team is a creative process which is located within individuals, albeit fostered sometimes by interaction processes in teams. In one study of 13 oil company teams, Caroline Burningham and myself found that individual propensity to innovate was superior as a predictor of team innovation (measured by reports from selected expert observers) to measures of group climate and process. Similarly, in a study of 435 health care workers, David Bunce and I found that individuals' tendency to innovate was a better predictor of changes in work role innovation over time than group climate factors.

The knowledge, skills and abilities (KSAs) of team members also influence outcomes – both domain-relevant KSAs (for example, the nurse's knowledge of her/his field) as well as team-functioning KSAs. Do team members have the KSAs necessary for effective teamwork?

THE TEAM TASK

Also important is the nature of the task that teams are required to perform. Tasks which demand a high degree of skill, which require team members to carry out a variety of different activities, and which involve the use of a number of different skills and talents are likely to produce high levels of team creativity. Task identity is also an important factor. This is the degree to which the job requires completion of a whole, identifiable piece of work and to which it involves doing a job from beginning to end. Teams charged with such tasks are more likely to be creative. Task significance also promotes team creativity; this is the degree to which the team task has a substantial impact on the lives of other people, whether these people are in the immediate organization, or in the wider commercial or social environment. Team task autonomy refers to the degree to which the team task provides substantial freedom, independence and discretion in scheduling the work and determining the procedures used in carrying it out. Task autonomy tends to be highly correlated with team creativity and innovation. Task feedback is the degree to which carrying out the work activity required by the team task provides team members with direct and clear information about the effectiveness of their performance. This will also contribute to a team's level of creativity and innovation. Overall, team task complexity and challenge are likely to demand innovation from team members.

But understanding group performance requires careful consideration of the group's organizational context. Indeed, researchers are increasingly pointing towards the role that the organization plays in determining group effectiveness. Sufficient resources, appropriate training and information systems, group-based rewards, and assistance to the team in its functioning are all seen as important organizational factors affecting the performance of groups in organizations. It is this group of factors which we will consider next.

RESOURCES

It is often assumed that the level of team innovation is determined by the resources available to the team and, by extension therefore, the *slack* resources available within the organization. However, there is one seam of evidence which suggests that resources are not related to levels of team innovation. In a major United Nations study of research team effectiveness it was concluded that:

> *there was no evidence that more resources and better facilities led necessarily to better scientific performance. Once there was sufficient to employ good people in reasonable facilities there was little additional effect of throwing more money at the research problem (at least on average!)* (Payne, 1990)

In a study of innovation in top management teams of the British National Health Service hospitals, conducted by Neil Anderson and myself, we also found that levels of resources were unrelated to innovation (West and Anderson, 1996).

ORGANIZATIONAL CLIMATE

The climate of the organization in support of innovation and team working is also important to group innovation. A number of educational and industrially-based studies have demonstrated that a climate supportive of innovation facilitates effective team innovation. In a study of 54 manufacturing organizations conducted by myself and colleagues, we found that innovative organizations had climates characterized by an emphasis on quality, good communication, team working, interdepartmental co-operation, a preparedness to adapt to new demands, support for new and improved ways of doing things, and a strong tendency to constantly review and modify practices. For example, one automotive company that we visited had introduced extensive teamworking and very effectively so. However, on our second visit we found that the style of team-working had been changed dramatically. The managing director informed us that they had changed the approach simply because they were anxious that it would become too habitual!

ORGANIZATION SIZE

There is debate about whether innovation is more prevalent in small or large organizations, though there is a considerable body of evidence which suggests that large, dominant firms tend to innovate more, partly because they have the ability to raise finance to do so. On the other hand, there is also evidence that it is small, flexible firms which innovate most in the private sector. The paradox is unresolved. It seems safe to assume that innovation can be encouraged in any organization, regardless of size, given the appropriate circumstances.

This brief examination of influencing factors suggests that building an innovative team requires four to ten creative, innovative team members in an organization which is supportive (both rhetorically and practically) of innovation. The team should have diverse members (in terms of personality, professional background and views) and should not stay together more than three years. Their task should be challenging and important, and they should be given sufficient autonomy to get on with the job in their own way as well as given clear information on the effectiveness of their performance. Having established such a team, how can it then be helped to develop and implement creative ideas?

PROMOTING TEAM CREATIVITY

I will now describe various techniques designed to help generate new and different ideas in any area of team work activity. However, it is important to recognize that these techniques are simply aids and are not themselves magical sources of solutions. Creativity is 95 per cent hard work and 5 per cent fortunate discovery. Therefore, when teams use these techniques it is necessary to put in a good deal of effort to see how the ideas generated can help practically in dealing with the situation the team faces. What will not work is a passive approach which assumes that the right answers will just appear as a result of using the techniques.[1]

GOAL ORIENTATION

The goal orientation technique which is useful at the problem exploration and clarification stage involves critically examining and challenging targets and goals and can also be used for re-examining the ways in which problems and ideas are defined. This is invaluable in encouraging team members to identify and challenge basic assumptions which are often taken for granted. The approach leads to the framing of new targets and goals, and there are usually many more than were originally identified by the team. The formula of preceding goals with the words 'How to...' 'I wish...' is helpful for clarifying goals. Try to list as many 'How to...' and 'I wish...' as possible. Then the team should decide which are the most desirable, important, necessary, creative, visionary, practical, attainable, and begin to develop practical action plans to try to achieve them.

> **Example: How to deal with traffic jams:**
> **How to** reduce the number of cars on the road.
> **How to** get bigger roads.
> **I wish** we could get rid of traffic altogether.

---

[1] These techniques represent only a very small sample of those which can be used by team members to develop creative ideas. For an excellent description of creativity techniques which can be used by individuals or teams see Van Gundy, 1988.

How to get instant teleporting.
How to stop travel.
I wish we could shrink cars.
How to control traffic flow.
How to get lots of people in each vehicle.
I wish we could co-ordinate travelling plans.
How to always go by plane.
I wish I could hitchhike everywhere.

CLASSICAL BRAINSTORMING

This well-known approach is most useful at the idea generation phase of creative problem-solving. In classical brainstorming, team members produce as many ideas as possible, even Utopian or fantastic ideas. The aim is to produce a large quantity of ideas, not necessarily to worry about quality. Judgements are suspended and participants are urged to accept all ideas offered. Team members are also encouraged to use each other's ideas to stimulate more new ideas – this is called 'piggy-backing'. So the essential guide-lines are:

- quantity of ideas
- judgements suspended
- piggy-backing.

There are a number of ways in which brainstorming can be conducted in teams. One is to go round the team asking each member in turn for an idea, thus encouraging quieter group members to participate. Many prefer a less structured approach, however, where team members call out ideas randomly. However, the best way to conduct brainstorming is to give team members an opportunity to generate ideas alone and to write them down before bringing them to the team setting. At this point piggy-backing can occur. The advantage of everyone returning to the team is that it can bring team members together in fruitful social interaction, and confers a sense of participation and involvement in the generation of new ideas for change.

Classical brainstorming is used by many teams, but the most frequent mistake is the failure to suspend judgement while ideas are being proposed. During the idea-generation phase of problem-solving, critical judgement must be withheld. It is also valuable to encourage new, quite different, or even wild ideas in the brainstorming process, rather than brainstorming simply within the current paradigm of the team. Above all there should be an element of fun in brainstorming. It is sometimes the wildest and funniest ideas that contain within them the seed of a productive new approach to the task or issue which the team is facing.

BRAINWRITING POOL

This technique is a variant of classical brainstorming which builds on the superior performance of individuals over groups in brainstorms and has the effect of generating very large numbers of ideas, within a short space of time. Group members, seated around a table, are given blank sheets of paper with space to record ideas. After generating five or ten ideas the sheets are placed in the middle of the table. Each member then continues writing more ideas on the sheets filled in by other team members. They are urged particularly to piggy-back upon the ideas that others have already developed. A session of 20 minutes can produce hundreds of ideas from within a team. Redundancy is reduced because all participants can see the ideas produced by others. Furthermore, team members, while receiving stimulation from the ideas of other members of the team, can proceed at their own pace.

'Brain-netting' (a computer-based variant) involves setting up a file in a computer network system to which all team members have access. The problem or issue is headlined at the top of the file and then team members simply add their ideas or suggestions to those of their colleagues within the file. Team members do not need to be together to conduct the brainstorm and moreover, they all have a record of the ongoing outcomes of the process. This is a highly productive process which involves a minimum of effort from team members.

THE 'YES, AND...' METHOD

People often look for faults in a new idea when it is first raised. This can have the effect of reducing enthusiasm and the preparedness of people to offer new ideas. The 'Yes, and ...' method is a way of avoiding the negativity which is often the end of a new idea. Try saying 'Yes', and then building on the idea in a meeting before deciding that it will not work. Try to add your own positive idea to the suggestion. This is a simple but very powerful technique, which, if applied as a rule in departmental meetings, can change the climate substantially.

TABLE OF ELEMENTS

Another method for generating ideas during the 'ideation' phase of problem solving is the table of elements. This is a technique for breaking a problem or issue down into a set of elements or components, brainstorming within each, and then choosing from among the various components those ideas which seem most promising or creative in taking the team forward. It generates an enormous number of potential solutions to a problem in a very short space of time. However, it is only suitable for problems or issues which can be broken down into components and elements.

Example: the team has tried to come up with an idea for a novel social event which will bring people together and help them to have a good time outside work. The elements of this problem could be identified as:

> the people who will come to the event
> where the event will be held
> what activities will take place
> when the event will be held
> what the purpose of the event will be

The group then brainstorms ideas under each of these elements, or headings (see *Table 1* on p. 65). The next stage involves choosing potentially wild or promising ideas from among the many combinations of possibilities generated by the table of elements. In this exercise it is worth throwing in quite different ideas within each part of the brainstorm in order to enable team members to break out of existing ways of thinking. Participants can also choose an array of items from within the elements purely at random for example, by sticking a pin in each column to produce a novel combination). Inevitably, such strategies generate solutions which may appear outlandish or nonsensical at first sight. The purpose of these exercises however, is to stimulate new ways of looking at problems and this provides 5 per cent of the creativity. The other 95 per cent comes from the team in seeking to make the wild idea into a workable option.

For example, if the following items are selected from *Table 1:*

> – *children only*
> – *Bahamas*
> – *treasure hunt*
> – *weekend*
> – *learning to swim*

Table 1: Table of elements: A novel social event.

People	Place	Activities	Time	Purpose
Team members	Restaurant	Raise money for charity	Weekend	Learning to swim
Team members and partners	Park	Get to know each other	Friday evening	
Children only	Boat	Have a good time		
Team members and customers	Paris	As a reward		
Handicapped children	Bahamas	Treasure hunt		
Partners only	Motorway	Learn new language		
Team members' pets	Beach	Play golf		
	Swimming pool	Play tennis		
	Hotel			
	Theatre			

it is possible to combine them into the following more practical solution:

> Hold the social event as a treasure hunt for adults, which is spread over the afternoon, evening and morning of a week-end. The end of the treasure hunt on the first evening is located at an exotic hotel, where the theme of the food and refreshments is the Caribbean. On the following morning, the treasure hunt ends at a swimming pool where team members' children have been treated to swimming lessons, pool games and a lunch party.

NEGATIVE BRAINSTORMING

Negative brainstorming is a particularly useful technique for promoting excellence and critical thinking in teams and is most appropriate at the selection phase of creative problem solving. It can be used for testing a new proposal, or for evaluating an existing strategy, practice or objective. The technique involves the following three stages:

Step 1: Once a promising idea has been proposed (or in the case of an existing practice, the practice or strategy has been clearly identified), the team brainstorms around all possible negative aspects or consequences of the idea. This brainstorming should be as uninhibited as positive brainstorming in the classical approach. The intention is to generate a list of all the possible negative aspects of the idea or strategy, no matter how wild or fanciful these possibilities might appear.

Step 2: Team members choose four or five of the most salient criticisms, and examine these in more detail. At least one of these criticisms should be a wild or fanciful criticism.

Step 3: The team then considers how the idea or existing practice could be modified to deal with each of the criticisms in turn. This third stage of the process is essentially constructive, in that the team is seeking to build on a new or existing practice in order to counter the major criticisms of it.

It may be that some fundamental weakness or difficulty is identified, which the group sees no way of overcoming. In this case, the idea or the existing practice may be abandoned. However, this is a benefit rather than a disadvantage of the process, since it enables teams to identify at an early stage any idea or approach which is likely to be unsuccessful.

This approach is useful when an idea has reached the adoption and implementation phase of decision-making. In addition to drawing out the weak points of an idea before it is implemented, it also encourages constructive criticism. People are sometimes inhibited in their criticisms for fear of causing offence, and this approach makes it clear that criticism is directed at ideas and practices rather than people. If it is used on a regular basis, 'criticizing ideas as a way of improving on them' becomes accepted by the group as good practice.

STAKE-HOLDER ANALYSIS

This is a useful method for exploring an issue in more depth and improving upon existing and proposed solutions just prior to implementation. It can be used at both the selection and implementation stages of creative problem-solving by teams, and it is based on the idea that people are much less resistant to changes, as long as careful and creative thought has been put into considering how those changes will affect them in practice. Stake-holders are all those interested individuals and groups, both internal and external to the team, who affect or who are affected by the team's objectives and practices.

The technique involves the team, or individuals within the team, acting as if they were each stake-holder group in turn, and considering all the advantages and disadvantages arising from team objectives, strategies, processes or proposed changes. All possible advantages and disadvantages in relation to the stake-holder group are listed (see the example on p. 68). Then the proposed objective or change is modified in order to minimize the disadvantages to the stake-holder group and/or maximize the advantages. This is done for every major stake-holder in turn.

Any final objective or proposed change can be strengthened by such careful consideration of its effects upon the various stake-holders. The technique may also alert the team to conflicts which can then be dealt with using appropriate conflict-handling techniques.

USING CREATIVITY TECHNIQUES IN TEAM MEETINGS

It takes courage to attempt to use these creativity techniques in team meetings. New ideas are often greeted with only half-hearted support, ridicule, or even outright resistance. All creativity and innovation involves taking risks, and if the team is persistent and confident in introducing the techniques, they will be helpful. It can be

STAKE-HOLDER ANALYSIS IN PRACTICE

1. Proposed change
A large primary health care team which has always been run along traditional lines has proposed that it will become a fund-holding practice, more like a self-governing team responsible for its own finances and administration. This proposal consti-tutes a major shift in team practice and philosophy. Who are the major stake-holders?

2. Identify stakeholders
Patients, patients' relatives and carers, practice nurses, doctors, other staff, the community, professional associations, practice administrators and managers.

3. Advantages and disadvantages of the change
Patients
Possible advantages: improved speed of service; improved quality of care; improved administration.
Possible disadvantages: the practice has more concern with money than with patients; competition may lead to poorer-quality care.

Doctors
Possible advantages: better facilities; quicker decision-making; more control over resources.
Possible disadvantages: loss of medical emphasis; administra-tors will be more concerned with money than with patient care; specialist areas and equipment will be neglected in the inter-ests of satisfying large-scale demand.

Practice Managers
Possible advantages: more power; better quality decision-making; clearer managerial responsibilities.
Possible disadvantages: greater accountability; need to generate income; conflict with hospitals or other fund-holding practices

4. Adapting the change
Having identified potential advantages and disadvantages from the point of view of each stake-holder group, the team then considers how the change can be modified to meet the various concerns, or how the process of change could be managed appropriately to reduce resistance.

useful to string together a number of these creativity techniques; how this is done is itself an opportunity to be creative. It is worthwhile remembering the importance of the four steps of problem-solving described in Chapter 2, when planning a team session – *exploration, 'ideation', selection,* and *implementation.* Techniques appropriate to these stages should therefore be chosen.

It is also helpful to think carefully about how time in group meetings will be used, as well as which creativity techniques will be tried. Sufficient time needs to be allocated for each technique so that the team is not too rushed and each technique can be used effectively. Teams need a facilitator who understands the use of the techniques and does the job of a facilitator, rather than dictates or controls. He or she should ensure that there are sufficient materials for recording ideas, such as flip charts and overhead projectors.

To help create the right sort of team climate for creativity, it is useful to agree some ground rules before getting started. These can be posted on a flip chart to act as a reminder throughout the session. Ground rules will vary according to the particular aims of the team, but a typical set of ground rules for a creative session might well include:

- Be concise
- Show interest and support
- Jot down all stray thoughts
- Suspend judgement
- Say 'Yes and ...', rather than 'Yes but ... '
- Take risks – include the unusual and strange

If the flow of ideas is drying up, try taking a creative break from the problem. There are numerous ways of doing this, such as word association games, going out for walks, or story-telling.[2]

CHAPTER SUMMARY

Group processes are of fundamental importance in influencing team innovation, particularly the clarity of team objectives and support for innovation. The level of involvement and participation in the team, the commitment to engaging in vigorous debate and exploration to

---

[2]To determine how innovative your team is, try completing the *Team Climate Inventory.* This questionnaire asks about the climate or atmosphere in your work group or team and can give a clear indication of the helps and hindrances to innovation in your team. Some items from the questionnaire are shown in *Appendix 1.*

produce excellent quality services or products, and the overall support for new and improved ways of doing things in the team are all vital.

Other factors which are important include diversity in the team. Although team diversity may create conflict, in terms of competing perspectives and aims, it is constructive conflict which is the well of much creativity within teams. There is also a need to renew the team's perspectives regularly by changes in membership, the encouragement of innovation, and reviews of team objectives, strategies and processes.

The organization of which the team is a part also plays a significant role in providing explicit and implicit support for new and improved ways of doing things. The extent to which it encourages conflict, debate and diversity; the extent to which mistakes are accepted rather than punished in the quest for new and improved ways of working; the support for teamwork; and the contribution of resources to teams to enable them to generate new and improved ways of working all impact upon the effectiveness of innovation attempts.

Imagination is more important than intelligence. Intelligence is about the past and the present, but imagination is about the future.
Albert Einstein

Chapter Five

Innovation in Organizations

Firms which are skilful at innovation, the successful exploitation of new ideas – will secure competitive advantage in rapidly changing world markets; those which are not will be overtaken.

This comment in the 1993 British Government White Paper, *Realising Our Potential,* underlines the challenge to promote innovation within organizations. One of the major difficulties is that organizations are institutions of control, designed to produce uniformity and standardization. Consequently, the drive for innovation is directly contrary to the forces of control which exist within organizations. How can organizational innovation be promoted? What factors in organizations are associated with innovation? These questions are now so important that governments around the world are diverting considerable research funding into finding answers in order that their national economies can remain competitive through innovation in world markets. How then can organizational innovation be encouraged? What are the factors which determine or facilitate organizational innovation? And indeed, what is organizational innovation?

Recent research has shown that organizational change is most effective when multiple elements or changes are introduced; that is, rather than trying to change one aspect of the functioning of an organization, it is necessary to change many aspects simultaneously and in an integrated way in order to bring about real change. For example, simply introducing a suggestion scheme into an organization is unlikely to increase overall levels of innovation. All aspects of organizational functioning have to be examined to assess the extent to which they support or inhibit organizational innovation. We shall

MEASURING INNOVATION IN MANUFACTURING
ORGANIZATIONS

In one study of innovation in manufacturing organizations, 233 directors and senior managers from 171 UK manufacturing companies participated in a postal survey of innovation (Pillinger and West, 1995). The companies ranged in size from 60 to 1,929 employees, and represented five industrial sectors: Engineering – 45 companies; Electronics – 12; Plastics and Rubber – 84; Food and Drink – 9; and a miscellaneous group – 21. A survey questionnaire was designed to measure innovation in six areas.

1. Products
Managers reported on the number of new products, percentage of production workers involved, and sales turnover accounted for by the new products; this also included adaptation of existing products. Ninety-one per cent of the manufacturing companies had introduced new products over the previous two years and these accounted for, on average, 15 per cent of current sales turnover. However, only 7 per cent of companies were rated as 'moderate' to 'very high' on product innovation.

2. Production Technology
This concerned the introduction of new machines and/or systems such as computerized numerical control and single cycle automatic machines. Over 60 per cent of companies introduced new production technology. Most of the reported innovations were highly specific, such as the introduction of dowling machines. A quarter of companies further automated their plants with 15 per cent introducing CNC/DNC machinery. Sixteen per cent of companies were rated as 'moderate' to 'very high' on innovation in production technology.

3. Production techniques or procedures
Innovations in this area included the introduction of new information and planning systems, just-in-time and quality improvement. More than 70 per cent of companies had introduced new production techniques or procedures. The most frequently cited innovation was the implementation of TQM (Total Quality Management). Other popular innovations included the introduction of planning and control systems and further quality initiatives, such as the introduction of BS5750. Twenty-one per cent of companies were rated as 'moderate' to 'very high' on innovation in production techniques or procedures.

continued

continued _

4. Work organization
This area referred to the allocation of tasks and responsibilities across different groups of employees. Examples included multi-skilling, job rotation and cellular manufacturing. Seventy-five per cent of the companies had introduced changes in work organization over the previous two years. These included the introduction of team working and changes to company structure. Sixteen per cent of companies were rated as 'moderate' to 'very high' on innovation in work organizations

5. Human resource management (HRM)
HRM is concerned with issues such as recruitment and selection, induction, training and industrial relations. Managers described innovations introduced by their company in these five areas over the previous two years, the impact they had and how novel they were for the company (the results of this research are described later in this chapter). Over 66 per cent of companies have introduced changes in their human resource management systems over the previous two years. The most common innovations were in the areas of training and development, organizational communication and performance appraisal. Thirteen per cent of companies were rated as 'moderate' to 'very high' on innovation in human resource management.

This research suggests that innovation in organizations spans every area of their operations, and that innovativeness should therefore be measured in terms of products and services, management of people, information, communication and control systems, as well as ideas for new markets, services and directions.

Overall the findings from this research reveal that the level of innovation in organizations tended to be very low, with only minor innovations being introduced. (Pillinger and West, 1995.)

now look at a number of important organizational characteristics and practices which influence and increase innovation. They include: *organizational (or market) environment, culture, climate, organizational structure, competitive strategies, production or service technology, work design, emphasis on quality, human resource management practices, industrial relations, equal opportunities, research and development* (see *Figure 3*).

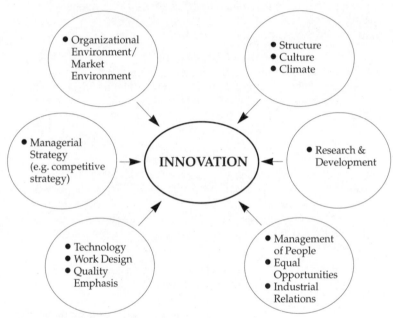

Figure 3: Major factors influencing organizational innovation.

MARKET ENVIRONMENT

Organizations are required to be innovative to the extent that their environment is unpredictable, unstable or threatening. Factors which influence the dynamic nature of the environment include the number of competitors, and in order to keep up with, or stay ahead of, this competition, organizations need to develop new and improved processes, services, products or organizational structures. Where market share is about the same or less than competitors, there is generally a need to develop new products and services or reduce costs. *Exercise 14* offers a questionnaire assessment of your organization's environment.

HOW UNCERTAIN IS YOUR ORGANIZATION'S ENVIRONMENT?

EXERCISE 14

The following questions refer to the degree of dynamism in the environment of your organization and give some indication of the requirement for innovation. The higher your total score (especially above 35), the more requirement there is for innovation.

(i) Actions of competitors are quite easy to predict (as in some primary industries).

Actions of competitors are very unpredictable.

1   2   3   4   5   6   7

(ii) Demand and consumer tastes are fairly easy to forecast (e.g. for a milk company).

Demand and tastes are extremely unpredictable.

1   2   3   4   5   6   7

(iii) The technology of the product/ service or production process is not subject to very much change and is well established (e.g. in steel production).

The technology of the product/service or production process changes often (e.g. advanced electronic components).

1   2   3   4   5   6   7

(iv) In this industry, organizations try to co-operate and co-exist with competitors.

A tough 'undo the competitors' philosophy is pursued in this industry. The industry is very competitive and hostile.

1   2   3   4   5   6   7

(v) In this industry, finding an ongoing supply of suitable labour does not present a problem.

Finding suitable people is proving very difficult in this industry.

1   2   3   4   5   6   7

continued

continued _____

(vi)   Profitability of firms in the market is very high with most of the firms making a lot of money.

        The average profitability of firms in the market is very low (e.g. most of the firms in the industry are losing money).

          1   2   3   4   5   6   7

(vii) Entry barriers in the market are very low (e.g. many new competitors have entered or may potentially).

        Entry barriers are very high. It is very difficult for new competitors to enter the market.

          1   2   3   4   5   6   7

(viii) In this industry, it is very difficult to differentiate products either physically or perceptually. They are commonly alike.

        There is considerable scope to differentiate products/ services in terms of quality, customization, image etc.

          1   2   3   4   5   6   7

(ix)   The markets that you serve are very homogeneous (e.g. a single undifferentiated market and very similar customers).

        The markets are very heterogeneous (e.g. a great diversity of markets, types of customers, etc).

          1   2   3   4   5   6   7

(x)   The industry is very concentrated, dominated by firms with large market shares who are able to strongly influence the competitive situation.

        The industry is extremely fragmented. No firm has a significant market share and the power to influence industry events.

          1   2   3   4   5   6   7

(Adapted from the interview schedule developed by the Corporate Performance Programme, Institute of Work Psychology, University of Sheffield.)

ORGANIZATIONAL CULTURE

Culture may be defined as the basic, taken-for-granted assumptions and deep patterns of meaning shared by organizational participation and manifestations of these assumptions, (Slocum, 1995). Organizational culture has major constraining or facilitating effects on the successful implementation and maintenance of innovation within organizations. Because it is such a difficult concept to capture and describe, it is first necessary to identify the basic elements of predominant cultures within organizations. Two fundamental dimensions of organizational culture are *flexibility* versus *control,* and *internal* versus *external* orientation.

Organizations have employed a variety of different structures to deal with the increasing complexity of the environment. These structures can be seen to form a continuum, ranging from those which are control-oriented to those which are oriented towards flexibility. High flexibility is characterized by flatter organizational structures, decentralized decision-making and low specialization of jobs, while high control cultures tend to be very hierarchical in their structures, with centralized decision-making and many specialized jobs with a proliferation of job titles. The appropriate structure in an organization should, of course, reflect the demands placed on it by the external environment. However, structures once established are difficult to change even when they have become part of a culture which may not serve the current environment. In an organization characterized by high control, in contrast, procedural rules are outlined and strictly adhered to; difficulties are resolved through a hierarchy; the organization chart rarely changes; knowledge is held at the top of the organization; the majority of communications are vertical; and supervisors give instructions rather than advice and information.

Another important indicator of the culture of an organization is the way it relates to the external world. Organizations can be distributed along a continuum from highly internally-oriented to highly externally-oriented. Internally-oriented cultures are characterized by a concern with what goes on within the organization and where the predominant focus of managerial and strategic effort is towards managing the organization internally. An external orientation is more concerned with customers, markets, acquisition of scarce resources and scanning of the organization's environment. Externally-oriented organizations are eager to learn from current practice in other organizations. Competitive activity is monitored closely; there are formal systems which involve clients in the design of services; much communication is directed towards projecting an organizational image externally; and many staff are involved in liaising with external groups or organizations.

Quinn and colleagues (1990) have combined the control and orientation dimensions to form the *Competing Values Framework* (see *Figure 4*). This is used to describe four competing cultural orientations, found in all organizations.

HUMAN RELATIONS

Organizations with predominantly human relations-oriented cultures are characterized by a concern that employees be committed, that levels of job satisfaction and employee well-being are high, and that there is a high level of skill development to maximize people's potential. The process of managing emphasizes participation, openness, discussion and consultation. Belonging and trust are core values. Leaders tend to be considerate and supportive, and they facilitate interaction and ownership through teamworking. There is a strong emphasis on training and personal development within the organization as a whole.

OPEN SYSTEMS

Here the emphasis is on flexibility and change. The primary concern of the organization is its ability to adapt quickly and appropriately to its environment. Roles and processes exist specifically to keep the organization in touch with the outside world. The organization places high values on the innovativeness of its employees. Resource acquisition is also given high priority, in terms of getting appropriate supplies, the appropriate workforce, winning financial backing and discovering the needs of customers and the activities of competitors. Leaders tend to be entrepreneurial, willing to take risks and able to develop and communicate a vision of the future. Characteristics include growth, stimulation, creativity and variety.

RATIONAL GOAL

Rational goal-based cultures emphasize productivity and achievement of goals. Planning, goal clarification, direction and decisiveness are characteristics of this type of culture. Managers are concerned with meeting the needs of customers, particularly to satisfy their orders in terms of timeliness and quality. Most performance indicators are related to profitability and productivity. Leaders tend to be

STRUCTURE

Flexibility

	Human Relations Model Goal Values: Human Resource Development Subgoals: Cohesion, morale, training	**Open Systems Model** Goal Values: Growth, resource acquisition Subgoals: Flexibility, readiness, external evaluation
FOCUS	**Internal**	**External**
	Internal Process Model Goal values: stability, equilibrium Subgoals: information management, communication	**Rational Goal Model** Goal values: productivity, efficiency, profit Subgoals: planning, goal setting

Control

Figure 4: The Competing Values Framework.

directive, goal-oriented and instrumental. Organizational structures tend to be functionally-based, and communication takes place through the hierarchy. Decisions are made at levels far removed from day-to-day operations. There is a sense of pressure to achieve within the organization. Employees usually receive well-focused job training, and individual performance measurement processes are much in evidence.

INTERNAL PROCESS

Organizations which have an internal process culture have well-developed information and control systems. There is a preoccupation with rules, regulations, and formal procedures. Managerial control systems are well developed and much training time is devoted to ensuring that control systems are understood and adhered to. Leaders tend to manage by report – stress is placed on measuring inputs rather than outputs. Leaders tend to be cautious and conservative in decision-making. Motivating factors in this type of culture largely reflect a need for security, stability and order.[3]

[3]Note – a fuller explanation of the Quinn model can be found in Quinn *et al.* (1990).

Organizations with cultures predominantly in the top half of the *Competing Values Framework* find the implementation of innovation easier to manage than those where the culture is predominantly rational goal- or internal process-orientated. This is partly because they already have many of the required features in place. For example, styles of management and team-based matrix type structures enable flexibility and change. In flexible organizations there is much less resistance to doing things differently.

However, if an organization's profile is predominantly in the bottom half of the framework, there is a need to allow longer timescales for the introduction of changes to encourage organizational innovation. There is also likely to be considerable resistance from those who fear loss of control, particularly personal control of their own environment. Of course, no organization lies totally within one section of the framework. There are differences between groups and differences between individuals within groups. However, the predominant culture within an organization will have established structures which reinforce that culture.

Some research evidence suggests that the most effective organizations have relatively balanced cultures; that is, they have satisfactory levels of internal process-orientation and rational goal-orientation but considerable emphasis is also placed on human relations and open systems. Non-innovative organizations characteristically have cultures weak in the latter two domains.

ORGANIZATIONAL CLIMATE

In addition to influencing structural design choices, either appropriately or inappropriately, organizational culture also affects the climate into which innovation is introduced. The climate of an organization refers to the overall functioning of the organization from the employees' points of view. It is the answer to the question 'What is it like to work here?' Climate is therefore a metaphor which describes the aggregate of individual employees' perceptions of their organization environment, a perception which influences their motivation and their innovation and performance.

Certain dimensions of climate particularly impact upon an organization's ability to successfully introduce innovation. These include *communication, participation, interdepartmental co-operation, support for innovation* and *reflexivity*. These can be assessed using the questionnaire in *Exercise 15*.

ORGANIZATIONAL CLIMATE

EXERCISE 15

The following questionnaire examines dimensions of climate which affect organizational innovation. Ask 10 to 20 people within your organization to complete the questionnaire, to give you an idea of their perceptions of the working environment or climate.

Circle the number which represents how much you agree with each statement in relation to the organization within which you work.

	Strongly disagree	Disagree	Neither agree nor disagree	Agree	Strongly agree
INNOVATION					
1. Assistance in developing new ideas is readily available in this organization.	1	2	3	4	5
2. This organization provides practical support for new ideas and their application.	1	2	3	4	5
3. In this organization, time is not given to develop ideas.	1	2	3	4	5
4. This organization never searches for new ways of looking at problems.	1	2	3	4	5
REFLEXIVITY					
1. In this organization objectives are modified in light of changing circumstances.	1	2	3	4	5
2. The methods used by this organization to get the job done are often discussed.	1	2	3	4	5
3. Organizational strategies are rarely changed.	1	2	3	4	5

continued

continued _____

	Strongly disagree	Disagree	Neither agree nor disagree	Agree	Strongly agree
4. In this organization, time off is not taken to review organizational objectives.	1	2	3	4	5

PARTICIPATION

1. Management involves people when decisions are made that affect them.	1	2	3	4	5
2. People in this organization feel they can influence the decisions that concern them.	1	2	3	4	5
3. Changes in this organization are made without talking to the people involved in them.	1	2	3	4	5
4. People in this organization feel decisions are frequently made over their heads.	1	2	3	4	5

INTERDEPARTMENTAL RELATIONS

1. There is very little conflict between departments in this organization.	1	2	3	4	5
2. Collaboration between departments is very effective.	1	2	3	4	5
3. People are suspicious of other departments in this organization.	1	2	3	4	5
4. People in different departments in this organization are reluctant to share information.	1	2	3	4	5

QUALITY

1. This organization is always working to achieve the highest standards of quality.	1	2	3	4	5

_____ *continued*

continued _____

	Strongly disagree	Disagree	Neither agree nor disagree	Agree	Strongly agree
2. People in the organization believe that its success depends on high quality work.	1	2	3	4	5
3. This organization does not have a good reputation for high quality.	1	2	3	4	5
4. People in this organization are not very concerned with producing top quality work.	1	2	3	4	5

Adapted from the climate measure developed by the Corporate Performance Programme, Institute of Work Psychology, University of Sheffield (Lawthom *et al.,* 1996)

Organization Climate Questionnaire – SCORING

Mark your score for each section on the grid below with an X:

	Poor		Variable	Good	
INNOVATION Add the scores for questions 1 and 2 then subtract the scores for questions 3 and 4.	−8	−4	0	+4	+8
REFLEXIVITY Add the scores for questions 1 and 2 then subtract the scores for questions 3 and 4.	−8	−4	0	+4	+8
PARTICIPATION Add the scores for questions 1 and 2 then subtract the scores for questions 3 and 4.	−8	−4	0	+4	+8
INTERDEPARTMENTAL RELATIONS Add the scores for questions 1 and 2 then subtract the scores for questions 3 and 4.	−8	−4	0	+4	+8
QUALITY Add the scores for questions 1 and 2 then subtract the scores for questions 3 and 4.	−8	−4	0	+4	+8

ORGANIZATIONAL STRUCTURE

Researchers and theoreticians have consistently suggested that organizations with flatter, organic structures are more likely to encourage innovation than are organizations characterized by many hierarchical levels and a strong emphasis on control.

Another structural indicator of innovativeness is the degree of centralization of decision-making. To the extent that responsibility for decision-making is devolved to the 'coal face', it is more likely that innovation will occur. When people are given responsibility and freedom to make decisions about how work is done, they are likely to introduce their ideas for new and improved ways of working. *Exercise 16* enables an assessment of the extent to which decentralization is characteristic of companies. The research of my colleagues at the Institute of Work Psychology suggests that, in the manufacturing sector, many managers believe they have decentralized decision-making (West *et al.*, 1996). However, an examination of the nature of decisions which are devolved tends to reveal that real decision-making is largely confined to senior management.

COMMUNICATION

Communication facilitates innovation since the more that information is communicated in all directions – laterally, horizontally and vertically – the more likely it is that new and improved ideas will be generated. Sharing of information provides the data which may prompt an idea for a new approach, a questioning of existing practice, or a reaction of surprise on discovery of some salient bit of information that was hitherto unknown. Information fuels innovation, and organizations which share knowledge and information widely are much more likely to reap benefits from the innovative ideas of employees in response. Simple questions which can be asked about communication in organizations are; What methods are used to communicate information to employees?; Are there, for example, issues of company newspapers and if so, how frequently?; Are there written or oral briefings on organizational performance or other company issues to management? Are there written or oral briefings on organizational performance to others in the organization and if so how frequently? Answers to such questions reveal whether even basic communication systems are in place. Sadly, in many British organizations, they are not.

Organizations which encourage interaction between different

CENTRALIZATION OF DECISIONS

EXERCISE 16

Which is the lowest level in your organization which has the authority to take decisions – who can take action without waiting for confirmation from above?

	Operator or service provider	Supervisor	Manager	Manager reporting to Chief Executive	Chief Executive	Above Chief Executive
1. Spend unbudgeted money (more than £250)	1	2	3	4	5	6
2. Create a new job	1	2	3	4	5	6
3. Determine a new product/service	1	2	3	4	5	6
4. Determine the pricing of a new product/ service	1	2	3	4	5	6
5. Dismiss a member of staff	1	2	3	4	5	6
6. Decide which suppliers/ service providers are to be used	1	2	3	4	5	6
7. Decide whether to promote an employee	1	2	3	4	5	6
8. Select an applicant for a job	1	2	3	4	5	6

The more decision-making is concentrated at senior management levels, the less likely innovation at lower levels is to be encouraged.

functions, professions and specialisms are also likely to stimulate innovation as a consequence. Integration or structural liaison devices encourage innovation via cross-functional communication between departments. In order to ensure compatibility between decisions in one area of the organization with those in another area, it is important that such integrative methods are used. These can include inter-departmental groups/teams which are set up to allow departments to engage in joint decision-making; task forces or temporary bodies set up to facilitate interdepartmental collaboration on a specific project; cross-team memberships; and liaison personnel whose specific job it is to co-ordinate the efforts of several departments or teams for the purposes of, for example, a specific project.

COMPETITIVE STRATEGIES

Competitive strategies influence the extent to which innovation is encouraged within organizations. New approaches, such as business process re-engineering or redesign, the introduction of external training, and the use of consultancy services can have an impact on levels of innovation. Other competitive strategies which encourage innovation include:

- the intent to produce high quality services or products to distinguish the organization from competitors;
- giving better quality of service to customers in order to gain a competitive edge;
- being willing to adapt products or services to meet special customer needs;
- providing related products or services alongside core products or services to fulfil the complete needs of customers;
- trying to stay ahead of competitors in terms of service or product novelty;
- speed of innovation development;
- new plant, equipment and process improvements.

TECHNOLOGY

Innovation is both a cause and a consequence of the extent to which there is organizational commitment to exploring and exploiting new technology as a way of promoting organizational effectiveness. Innovative organizations are willing to try out new and improved technologies such as voice transcription on computer; voicemail; computer numerical control; computer-aided designs; computer-aided engineering and computerized production planning. Key questions are: Is the organization prepared to experiment with new technology in order to improve products and services?; Is the organization prepared to invest in developing new systems which exploit state-of-the-art enhancement of information use?; Does the organization tend to employ new technology only when it has been well-established and accepted in other organizations?

WORK DESIGN

In Chapters 3 and 4 we discussed the benefits of designing jobs and team objectives in ways which enhanced the motivating quality of the jobs while offering creative challenges to job incumbents or team members. Many members of the UK workforce are unskilled (at least in the workplace) and have jobs with a low level of responsibility, autonomy and accountability. It is unlikely that innovation will be fostered in organizations which perpetuate these job designs. In organizations characterized by high levels of work force skill and development, or where *multi-skilling* is widely used (that is, people can carry out a number of different roles within the organization as a result of having experienced the demands and challenges associated with different roles), innovation understandably is more frequent. Innovative organizations are likely anyway to practise *job rotation*, multi-skilling and encourage *cross-departmental collaboration* in order that employees can learn about the wider functions of the organization as well as the work of specific departments. Such organizations respond to the hunger for learning and competence which motivates so much of human activity.

One indication of the quality of work design for innovation is the typical time per task cycle in jobs – *job cycle time*. For example, in one manufacturing organization I observed two women packing stockings into a box. Each task cycle (the time taken to pack a pair of stockings) took approximately three seconds. As the women were paid according to the numbers of pairs of stockings they packed, the task cycle was extraordinarily short and very pressured. There is a similar short cycle amongst post office sorting staff, required to type correct postcodes for letters incorrectly coded. Here the task cycle time was approximately 1.2 seconds. Compare this with the cycle time likely

---

WHAT PREDICTS INNOVATION? CHALLENGE AND CO-ORDINATION

In a study of innovation in UK manufacturing described earlier (Pillinger and West, 1995), the results showed two characteristics associated with higher overall company innovation. These were low market share and team working. Companies with lower market share and those where teams rather than individuals had responsibility for work were more innovative overall. Team working is widely regarded as an effective vehicle for innovation, though of course it may be an innovation in itself for many companies. The most innovative companies also had good interdepartmental communication and co-operation, were more prepared to adapt to meet customer demands and needs, supported ideas for new and improved ways of doing things, and had a strong tendency to constantly review and modify practices. The results painted a picture of companies innovating in an evolutionary fashion adapting to external threat and demand but the report concluded that 'the challenge to these companies in the future is to develop innovative strategies designed to determine rather than simply respond to a changing market position'.

---

to be associated with carrying out a research project which could last for two or three years, or writing a book which might take six months. Longer cycle times are clearly associated with more opportunities for innovation. Very short cycle times produce boredom and stress.

Another influence on innovation is the *variety* in jobs. Conducting a research project offers almost infinitely more variety than packing stockings and typing post codes – hence also many more possibilities for innovation. So how could innovation be encouraged in those latter jobs? One way is simply to redesign the jobs so they involve more task elements. Another is to use job rotation as a way of encouraging variety and therefore the likelihood of innovation. As people experience different jobs within the organization they are more likely to offer useful ideas for improving organizational functioning.

Innovation is also encouraged by giving people at all levels responsibility for quality problems, material supply problems, machine or technology repair, determining when to take breaks and the order in which to do their work. The more responsibility people have at the lowest levels of the organization, the more likely it is that innovation will be encouraged.

One of my colleagues, Toby Wall, conducted research in a situation where machine operators were given responsibility for the routine maintenance of advanced manufacturing technology equipment (Wall and Jackson, 1995). Previously they had always been required to call engineers in for machine breakdown and routine maintenance. The introduction of greater responsibility and autonomy for workers had beneficial and unexpected effects. Not only was the downtime (the time for which they were not functioning) of the machines much shorter, but the *frequency* of the occurrence of downtime was reduced as well. It appears that operators were not only managing to maintain the machines in a way which enabled them to get the machines working again more quickly when they went down, but they were anticipating problems and preventing them from occurring in the first place. As a rule, when comparing across organizations doing similar work, the amount of technical knowledge required for the job at the lowest levels of the organization is a good indication of the extent to which responsibility has been devolved, and therefore of the extent to which innovation will be stimulated as a consequence.

QUALITY

One of the main findings from our research on service and manufacturing organizations is that emphasis on quality in organizations predicts innovation. An indication of the extent to which quality policies are implemented (and innovation is therefore likely to be encouraged), is whether and how quality is formally evaluated, for example, in terms of customer complaints, and defect rates. Of course, monitoring quality is of little value in itself, if these measures of quality performance are not communicated to the workforce both speedily and informatively. Moreover, training in quality issues for all levels of employee is crucial if quality is to be encouraged.

HUMAN RESOURCE MANAGEMENT (HRM)

How people are managed within organizations will influence their contribution to innovation within the organization. The commitment of the organization to human resource management is an indication of their human relations orientation, in terms of the Quinn and Cameron model described earlier. Yet, in many organizations (surprisingly) there is no-one with overall responsibility for personnel matters and the suggestion that personnel issues should best be managed by line managers is often used as an excuse for not addressing the HRM issues. This is a picture very different from that painted by the widespread discussions of HRM in the television and print media, business and management schools, and the management books in railway station bookstalls. Ideally, an organization should indicate its commitment to HRM by having one person on the board or at senior management level responsible for Personnel or Human Resource Management. The organization should also have a formal human resource strategy endorsed by the top management team which is translated into work programmes. The conduct of appraisal and career development reviews should also be included as a job requirement for managers within the organization. Aside from these broad strategic issues, what other aspects of HRM should be considered in designing organizational practices to encourage innovation?

RECRUITMENT AND SELECTION
The sophistication and value of recruitment and selection procedures indicates the extent to which the organization is committed to finding the most skilled and appropriate people. Where the sophistication of recruitment and selection procedures is low, it is likely that the organization is satisfied with minimal skill levels and therefore does not encourage effective innovation as a consequence. Limited forms of selection include simply seeking to fill vacant positions from amongst current employees, advertising internally, or using word of mouth. More extensive recruitment and selection would include advertising externally, the use of recruitment agencies, Job Centres and encouraging apprentices. Some researchers argue that managers tend to pursue an 'attraction-selection-attrition' approach, whereby they attract people very similar to those already in the organization; select those similar to themselves and employ unconscious practices which lead to the departure of those who are dissimilar from others in the organization. Such processes reduce diversity and hinder innovation.

Selection methods can include application forms, interviews, biodata, psychometric testing, work samples, references and aptitude

EMPHASIS ON QUALITY

EXERCISE 17

1. **How high is the level of involvement of all of the workforce in quality?** To what extent are operators/service providers responsible for monitoring and correcting quality problems? Do they have authority to make changes to meet quality criteria? How sophisticated are feedback mechanisms giving service providers/operators/all employees quick and accurate feedback on the quality of work?

1	2	3	4	5
Very low	Low	Neither high nor low	High	Very high

2. **How sophisticated is the approach to quality in your organization?** Does the organization have a written statement of quality policy? How well has the organization implemented initiatives such as BS5750, ISO9000, ISO9002, Investors in People?

1	2	3	4	5
Non existent	Poor	Neither good nor bad	Good	Outstanding

3. **How much effort is expended on improving quality in your organization?** How much money and time is committed to promoting quality in the organization, and how senior is the person/people responsible for quality policy? To what extent are substantial resources committed to training employees in quality/audit issues?

1	2	3	4	5
Very little	Little	Moderate	High	Very high

4. **How extensive is the emphasis on quality within your organization?** Does it relate to all aspects of the organization's work and functioning such as managing meetings, office environments, customer service, quality of services/products, telephone practices, published documents?

1	2	3	4	5
Very limited	Limited	Average	Extensive	Very extensive

tests. We know that interviews by one person, bio-data and references are very poor methods of predicting work performance. However, interview panels, psychometric testing, work sampling and the use of aptitude data can help considerably in the process. Of course, multiple methods are of most value, particularly if they are augmented by information about the person's on-the-job performance.

APPRAISAL

Where formal appraisal systems exist, focused on goal-setting and feedback on work performance, there is some evidence that performance improves as a result. However, appraisal systems are often confounded, with bonus setting payment systems and career development so obfuscating the central aim. Such multiple menu approaches to appraisal are relatively ineffective. Ideally an appraisal system should simply focus on co-operative goal-setting, and performance review against clear objectives and to specified and agreed criteria. Appraisal systems can also be assessed in terms of their application throughout the workforce – amongst management, professional, technical, clerical, administrative and shop floor workers. Their frequency should be a minimum of yearly and those conducting appraisals should receive formal training. Ideally, there should be no link between appraisals and remuneration, and considerable emphasis should be placed upon employees participating in setting performance targets and finding avenues of personal development. Finally, of course, it is important that there is some formal system to monitor whether appraisals have taken place as they should.

REWARDS

If the intent is to encourage innovation within organizations, then clearly reward systems should be geared towards encouraging innovation. At 3M (a tape manufacturing company), for example, employees are given 15 per cent of their time to conduct 'blue sky' projects (following their creative ideas), and are encouraged to act as 'pirates' within the organization, 'stealing' resources wherever they can to support the development of their innovation projects (3M developed the classic yellow stick-it notes through such processes). When they produce an innovation which looks to be a success, they are assigned to that project full time and reap some of the promotion and monetary rewards associated with its success. Notably, they are not punished for failures and mistakes. The use of employee share options, profit-sharing, group/company bonus schemes and team bonuses, can facilitate innovation, but are notoriously difficult to implement fairly in practice. Individual bonuses may often impede effective innovation unless they are tied legitimately and clearly to identifiable contributions to innovation. Also, where there are major discrepancies between the non-monetary benefits of shop floor and management staff, it is likely to decrease the commitment of shop floor staff and thereby also their innovation. These include benefits such as subsidized canteen, pensions, private health, flexitime, child-care and company cars.

LEARNING ORGANIZATIONS
A currently popular notion is the concept of the 'Learning Organization', which refers to organizations which have a commitment to growth, development, learning and creativity throughout the organization, as a means of achieving strategic advantage. Learning organizations encourage all employees to develop their skills and broaden experience and are more likely to be innovative than those which do not. Having a workforce with a wide range of developing skills is clearly more likely to encourage innovation than having a workforce whose skills are largely static. Learning organizations tend to have information on training courses that might be of value to employees readily available, and they have a formal recognized procedure by which employees meet with their managers/supervisors to discuss long term career development. They often arrange visits to external suppliers or customers for employees who would not normally have such contact as part of their normal job responsibilities. Employees working in one department are often seconded to another department so that they can learn more about the processes and procedures in that area. Many employees have an official role or a specific responsibility to coach and teach others relevant skills. There is often support for learning and training that is not work-related, such as language development, basic skills and even some hobbies. Training is generally available that is work-related but not directly necessary for the individual's current job – for example, learning about processes that occur in other parts of the organization or courses to increase computer skills. In learning organizations there is often a formally recognized mentoring system – a system where an employee has a named colleague who provides advice and guidance on a regular basis.

TRAINING

Innovative organizations almost always have well-developed, sophisticated and thorough training strategies. Usually there are minimum annual training requirements for all and managers are able to outline the main sorts of training taking place for shop floor, professional/technical, clerical and management employees. The average number of hours of training for a typical employee per year is likely to be high, at around 80 – 120 hours. The company is also likely to be financing external training for many employees. Underlying the approach to training in innovative organizations is a systematic strategy to analyse employee training needs, including analysis of project or business or service plans, training audits, performance appraisal and employee requests for training. The approach to training in such organizations is likely to be highly planned and organized rather than reactive or responding simply as demands arise.

INDUSTRIAL RELATIONS

There are three ways of viewing industrial relations in organizations – what might be called the *unitary* approach, the *political* approach , and the *radical* approach.

Unitarist approaches see organizations as ideally meeting the needs concurrently and harmoniously of all stakeholders – shareholders, customers, managers and employees. *Political* approaches recognize the inevitability of conflict, particularly between managers and employees, since the former represent the views of shareholders and may seek to hold costs (such as employee pay) down. Some who adopt the political approach argue that this conflict is a source of potential innovation in organizations, particularly when the views of differing groups are examined, debated and agreement is reached on an appropriate way forward. A more *radical* perspective sees employees as inevitably and necessarily opposed to managerial orientations which seek to restrict their freedom and exploit their resources. Whichever view is adopted, there is strong evidence that conflict, carefully worked through, can be a source of innovation in organizations. In some research, the extent of trade union representation is positively associated with innovation. There is no evidence that worker representation on top management boards leads to higher levels of organizational innovation or effectiveness. There is clear evidence, however, that the introduction of team-based working is, thus providing some support for the political perspective on organizational functioning.

EQUAL OPPORTUNITIES AND DIVERSITY

The more diverse the workforce, the more likely it is that an organization will be innovative, just simply because of the variety of alternative perspectives that are brought to bear. The widespread practice of discriminating against women in organizations therefore is a major drawback to innovation, and some research evidence indicates that the involvement of women in management and particularly in teams is associated with higher levels of innovation. By so systematically and dramatically discriminating against women, organizations are depriving themselves of the innovativeness which results from women's involvement in the workforce at management and professional levels. Moreover, professional diversity is associated with increased innovation in both teams and organizations. The greater the variety of cultural contributions to the intelligence of the organization, the more innovative the organization is likely to be. This argues therefore that equal opportunities within organizations is not simply a matter of moral good practice, but makes business sense as well. The conflict of perspectives generated by heterogeneity is the stuff of innovation; it is through managing the conflict and diversity associated with heterogeneity that creativity and innovation are generated.

RESEARCH AND DEVELOPMENT (R & D)

Economists tend to use measures such as R & D expenditure and number of patents as an indication of innovation in organizations. Research and development activities are clearly associated with innovation and the commitment of organizations to this area is important. However, in our research in manufacturing organizations we found often that there are no research and development departments and related expenditure is often low. Indeed, a major criticism often made of manufacturing organizations in Britain is that they fail to make a commitment to research and development.

On the other hand, one company in the oil and gas sector that I visited, was contributing 12 per cent of its sales to R & D expenditure.

It is one of the most innovative and successful organizations, albeit very small, in the area. There is a lesson here for many organizations, that despite their anxiety about investing money in unknown outcomes, the value of research and development in fostering innovation and therefore company performance has clearly been demonstrated by economists. Indeed some companies such as 3M aim to ensure that 60 per cent of their sales are accounted for by new products developed within the last three years.

CHAPTER SUMMARY

This swift gallop across the vast plains of organizational functioning can only skim over a few areas, leaving enormous tracts of territory uncovered. Each topic, briefly covered here, merits a book to itself. Even so, some of the main aspects of this organizational landscape have been identified and their contribution to innovation indicated. What research and theory so far suggest is that innovative organizations will have integrated structures, cultures and practices, such that the ideas and commitment of those who work within them are nurtured and rewarded. Cultures are open, flexible and supportive – the emphasis is on what can be done, not what cannot. The climate is one of liberalism, autonomy, supportiveness, openness and careful risk taking, where communication and co-operation across boundaries are valued and encouraged. Innovation is sought out and enabled with the provision of resources, facilities and time. Jobs are designed to develop the people who carry them out, and quality is celebrated and rewarded in all domains of organizational activity. People are encouraged to set targets in their work and they receive clear feedback on their performance. Employee welfare and well-being are concerns of all associated with the organization, and diversity of the workforce in terms of gender, professional background, race, national culture, training, personalities and tenure in the organization, is valued. Conflict is seen as an important contributor to organizational life, like the grit in the oyster which produces the pearl. But it is well managed, constructive and quite different from the hideous interpersonal conflicts and power struggles of pathological organizations. Teamwork is the preferred way of working in innovative organizations and it is practised intelligently, not just rhetorically. These innovative organizations do exist though they are rare features of the organizational landscape. What is lacking in many organizations is the courage of individuals at senior levels to take these innovative ways of managing and implement them in their own organizations.

Do what you are afraid to do. When you run away because you are afraid to do something big, you pass opportunity by.
W. Clement Stone

It is the greatest of all mistakes to do nothing because you can only do a little. Do what you can.
Sydney Smith

Chapter Six

Managing Innovation

...There is no more delicate matter to take in hand, nor more dangerous to conduct, nor more doubtful in its success, than to set up as a leader in the introduction of changes. For he who innovates will have for his enemies all those who are well off under the existing order of things and only luke warm supporters in those who might be better off under the new. This luke warm temper arises partly from the fear of adversaries who have the laws on their side and partly from the incredulity of mankind who will never admit the merit of anything new, until they have seen it proved by the event.
Niccoló Machiavelli, *Le Prince*

The ultimate measure of a man is not where he stands in moments of comfort and convenience, but where he stands at times of challenge and controversy.
Martin Luther King

So far we have explored the factors which facilitate individual, team and organizational innovation. We have considered how influencing factors can determine levels of individual creativity, the extent to which a team develops and implements innovation, and the overall innovativeness of whole organizations. In this chapter we shall examine how to manage the processes of implementing innovation within organizations. As Machiavelli suggests, the process is likely to have as fellow travellers conflict and, consequently, unpopularity. It needs careful planning.

THE INNOVATION PROCESS

Based on his analysis of over 3,000 studies of organizational innovation, Everitt Rogers (1983) described the innovation process as consisting of two major stages: *initiation* and *implementation*. These in turn have two and three sub-stages respectively which are described below. Effective implementation of innovation is more likely when the innovator plans the management of each stage thoughtfully and realistically.

1. The initiation process – the start of innovation

Sub-stage 1: Agenda setting. Agenda setting refers to the identification of organizational problems where there is a mismatch between the actual and desired performance of the organization or some part of it. As a result of problem identification, innovation can be stimulated in one of two major ways. First, a specific performance gap may be noticed, such as dissatisfaction with the management of customer complaints. An innovation may then be introduced as a consequence of recognition of this gap; for example, improved training for those responsible for managing customer complaints.

Another means of agenda setting is through organizational members becoming aware of a practice in another organization which, if adopted, would enable them to overcome a problem in their own organization. In the course of complaining about service as a customer to an electrical goods department, a manager of an automotive parts company might find that she is given a very helpful response by the electrical goods company. Not only is she given a new piece of equipment in place of the faulty equipment she had purchased, but subsequently she receives a letter of apology and a reassurance of good intent from the manager of the electrical goods company. This may prompt her to initiate a similar set of practices within the company which she manages. This may then help to minimize the problem of customer complaints. Rogers terms these two different ways of stimulating innovation, *'problem initiated'* and *'innovation initiated'* innovation processes.

Sub-stage 2: Matching. In this stage, judgements are made about how likely the identified innovation is to meet the specific problem facing the organization. On the basis of these judgements the innovation process is either terminated or continued. It is a process of constructively appraising and criticizing the idea to determine its real value in meeting organizational needs.

2. Implementation stage

Sub-stage 1: Re-defining/re-structuring. The innovation to be adopted is modified or reinvented to fit the specific requirements of the organization. The automotive parts company may have only a small number of customers and so formal letters of apology might not be appropriate. Telephone calls or personal visits to customers from the managing director, apologizing for problems, might be deemed a more powerful and effective strategy for handling customer complaints. Alternatively, aspects of the organization may be altered to fit the innovation. Thus, if there was no customer complaints desk in the organization, a location might be used to provide such a service and appropriate jobs created.

Sub-stage 2: Clarifying. The innovation is implemented and discussed fully with employees in order that its meaning is made clear to all affected by it. Where misunderstandings arise about the purpose or the content of the innovation, further information is supplied. Where there are unanticipated side effects then corrective action is taken.

Sub-stage 3: Routinizing. In the routinizing sub-stage, the innovation becomes part of the normal organizational process and has reached a point where it is no longer identified as being an innovation. It is a routine, accepted part of organizational functioning.

Rogers argues that generally the later stages of the process cannot successfully be completed if the earlier ones have not also been negotiated. There may be backtracking from one point of the process to another, for example from re-defining/re-structuring to matching, but in general the process tends to be linear.

A simpler representation of the innovation process is offered by Richard Daft (1992), who sees the innovation process as involving five stages or elements.

1. Needs

A performance gap is recognized and innovation alternatives are considered.

2. Idea

An idea for a new and improved way of doing things is generated. The idea is then matched to the need.

3. Adoption

Adoption occurs when decision makers decide to support the implementation of the proposed idea for implementation.

4. Implementation

Implementation occurs when organizational members begin to use a new idea, technique or process in practice, in their work.

5. Resources

The final element is the human energy and activity required to bring about the change. Daft argues that change requires time and resources to be dedicated to creating and implementing ideas and that resources are therefore vital in the process of innovation.

Daft believes that for a change to be successfully implemented, each of the five elements must occur within the organization. If one of the elements is missing the change will not be implemented effectively.

INNOVATION AND CONFLICT

As suggested in Machiavelli's observation at the beginning of this chapter, the innovation process is inevitably associated with psychological or interpersonal conflict. If a new way of doing things is introduced within an organization and no conflict is generated (that is, there are no disagreements about the content or process of the innovation), or if there is no resistance by organization members to the innovation, then this innovation is not really new, nor does it offer a significant contribution to the organization. *Innovation threatens the status quo and thereby produces conflict.*

CHARACTERISTICS OF INNOVATION

Innovations can be judged in terms of their *magnitude* – the size of the innovations and their likely impact. The bigger an innovation, the more it will bring about change and conflict and threaten people's positions within the organization.

- *Novelty* is the newness of the innovation to the organization. For example, in an organization that has traditionally managed work individually with associated promotion and reward systems, people will find the introduction of wide scale team-based working highly novel. Such novelty will generate considerable conflict.
- *Radicalness* is the extent to which an innovation represents a change to the status quo. Where an innovation involves substantial changes, for example to the power of departments, groupings

or managerial levels, it will generate conflict. If, for example, it is decided to devolve financial responsibility from the finance department down to functional units and teams such that they become responsible for their own budgets, the change to the status quo will produce resistance because of the diminution of the finance department's power. Threats to the status quo, resulting from the radicalness of innovations, are associated with greater conflict.

- *Effectiveness* refers to the likely effectiveness of innovations within organizations. Innovations are ultimately judged in terms of their likely contribution to the effectiveness of the organization. Where it is believed that the potential impact is likely to be damaging rather than helpful, greater conflict will be generated. Particularly where an innovation is seen as high risk there will be considerable conflict and resistance to the change.

Of course, innovations are only judged as innovations *after* they have been successfully implemented. Consequently, our judgements of innovation tend to be surrounded by a halo of positive expectations. The reality is that many innovations in organizations fail and sometimes with disastrous consequences. Nevertheless, for innovation to be developed some degree of risk taking must occur, and some tolerance of failures is necessary. Children learn to walk partly by falling down repeatedly!

RESISTANCE TO CHANGE

Managing innovation processes involves understanding the reasons why people resist change in organizations and recognizing that resistance to change is not necessarily good or bad. In some instances it is a normal and natural reaction to change. In other instances it is a reasonable reaction to an inappropriate attempt to change the status quo. Not all innovation and change is for the best, nor is it always well thought out. Resistance to change can be an important force for ensuring that change is introduced carefully. Let us look at some of the reasons why people resist change.

- *Parochial self interest*
  Sometimes change is just seen as inconvenient and people resist change because it *is* change, regardless of whether they perceive it to be to the benefit or detriment of the organization. They may also feel that the change will somehow be disruptive to their own work lives.

- *Vested interests*
  People resist change if they see it threatening their job security, power, status, pay differentials, or the diversity of their jobs. These are important reasons for resisting organizational change, and it is understandable and justified for people to resist threats to their basic job satisfactions, job characteristics and security. When introducing an innovation, it is essential to think through how the proposed change will affect other people within the organization, and what their reactions are likely to be.

- *Misunderstanding*
  A frequent cause of resistance to change is misunderstanding about the nature of the change and its consequences. This most often occurs when there is inadequate consultation and information-sharing about the innovations to be introduced. Consequently, suspicions and misunderstandings grow and people inevitably resist or even sabotage the innovation. Managing innovation effectively means informing very fully all those affected by, or who perceive they may be affected by, the innovation being introduced.

- *Low tolerance of change*
  People often resist change simply because they have endured too much over a given period of time. Colleagues within the British National Health Service (NHS) often argue that the amount of change they have experienced in recent years has been so great, so continual and so overwhelming that they feel a strong need for stability. Consequently, they will often resist change *whatever* its anticipated benefits.

- *The change process*
  Resistance to change is often a consequence of the mis-management of consultation, education and participation processes. If people are involved in the innovation process they are much less likely to resist the change. If it is perceived as necessary to introduce a change without any consultation or participation (perhaps because of time pressures), those involved in the innovation process should make their strategy and the reasons for this strategy sharp and clear to those affected by the change. This is likely to produce less resistance in the long run than engaging in a process of consultation for window dressing purposes only. Where people only appear to be involved in influencing decisions about change, and they repeatedly see their contributions

carrying little weight, the consultation process becomes devalued and ultimately ignored.

ORGANIZATIONAL RESISTANCE TO CHANGE – 'DEFENSIVE ROUTINES'

Organizations are not identifiable entities in their own right and are simply made up of individuals, but because of their scale and complexity they often seem like organisms and to have a personality and life of their own. One way in which scholars think about organizations is as organisms seeking to survive and developing mechanisms to survive in a changing environment. Just like living organisms, they develop immune systems to fight against attacks which threaten their survival or their form. These immune systems in one sense are found in the norms and unwritten rules of the organization and can be very difficult to detect. Where they are detrimental to the organization's long term effectiveness, these organizational defences are referred to as *defensive routines*. As routines they are set into motion automatically and often without deliberate intent on the part of any one individual.

Defensive routines are often designed to reduce difficulty and embarrassment within organizations and so can inhibit learning. Because they are designed to maintain the status quo, they often prevent the organization from dealing with the root causes of problems. They are one of the most important causes of failures in the implementation of innovations, because anything which threatens to change the status quo is likely to be dealt with as a virus and dealt with accordingly. Defensive routines are so closely entwined with organizations' norms, that they are undiscussable and their undiscussability is also undiscussable! Defensive routines make the unreasonable seem reasonable and are often disguised by being initiated in the names of caring and diplomacy. One example of a defensive routine is where people in an organization continually blame market conditions, political changes and economic circumstances for problems the organization is experiencing. Regardless of what goes on within the organization, problems are always explained in terms of what is occurring outside. Consequently, a kind of cohesion is maintained between people within the organization who collude together in not addressing their own performance problems.

Another example is denial of the existence of a problem in the first place. The organization might have before it the evidence of a market downturn in sales and orders, but senior managers keep dismissing this simply as 'blip' in the market, although the 'blip' is clearly, to any outside observer, a major precipice. Another example of this 'faking good' is an immediate reaction of crushing any suggestions for new and improved ways of doing things on the basis that it has been tried and failed elsewhere, or that it will cost too much, or that the initiator does not really understand the complexities of the situation. In some organizations, large numbers of people have survived by 'faking good' and marking time in their work. Innovation represents a threat to the cosy system they have created and is habitually resisted. Therefore, the reaction of those within such organizations is always to reject new ideas, but their reaction is undiscussable. Indeed, in such organizations, innovation is often promoted verbally, but in practice any attempt to introduce innovation is sharply thwarted. Suggestions for new ideas are tolerated and the innovator is placated by lukewarm words of support but without the practical follow-through of resources, time and real commitment.

A defensive routine which I and my colleagues frequently encounter in manufacturing organizations is one evoked in response to questions about implementation of human resource management and training strategies. It is argued that the organization has been under too much pressure to divert resources and attention towards these areas. Considerations about long-term strategies for the management of people have had to be put on one side, it is argued, in order to ensure the organization's immediate survival. The fact that so many organizations take this position suggests that many managers are unwilling to take human resource management seriously, either because they tend not to believe the rhetoric of psychologists and organizational scientists, or because they lack the expertise and confidence to manage people effectively. Yet the evidence is clear that those organizations which commit resources to developing enlightened people-management practices and improving job design, perform better financially than those which do not.

Exposing defensive routines is all the more difficult because they are so very hard to detect. People become immensely frustrated at the struggle involved in implementing a clearly sensible innovation, particularly when they are unable to understand why it is proving so difficult and why it arouses so much hostility. The following list gives some strategies for confronting defensive routines.

- Have arguments well thought out; reasons should be compelling, vigorous and publicly testable.

- Do not promise more than can be delivered; unrealistic promises can be seized upon to reject what is essentially a good idea.
- Be prepared to admit mistakes and then use them as a means of learning (for yourself and the organization).
- Always try to look beneath the surface. Continually ask 'Why?' of those who resist the change.
- Surface and bring into the open subjects which seem to be undiscussable, despite the hostility this may generate.
- Learn to be aware of when you are involved in, or colluding with, defensive routines.
- Try to see through the issues of efficiency (doing things right) to the more important questions of effectiveness (doing the right things). Unfortunately it is probably when you start asking questions at this level that most resistance is met. Such resistance may be an indication that you are close to identifying a defensive routine. Exposure of the defensive routine in the long run may help the organization, even though the person who exposes it may be seen as the problem, not a seeker for solutions. Machiavelli's comment about the loneliness of the innovator is strikingly accurate.

STRATEGIES FOR INTRODUCING INNOVATION

MINORITY INFLUENCE STRATEGY

Within social psychology in the last 20 years there has been an expansion of research and theorizing into how minorities exert influence over majorities. How did groups like the Greens and the Feminists bring about change in majority opinion when they began as minorities in conflict with majorities and those in power? A number of researchers have shown that minority consistency of arguments over time is likely to lead to change in the majority views. Charlan Nemeth, from the University of California at Berkley, has shown that while majorities bring about attitude change through public compliance, that is, the individual may first publicly conform to the majority view prior to internalizing that view, minority influence works in the opposite way (Nemeth and Staw, 1989). People exposed to a confident and consistent minority change their private views prior to expressing public agreement. This process has been labelled 'conversion' by minority influence researchers. A persistent, vocal minority which presents a coherent case for change, despite resistance, can bring about change in the attitudes and behaviour of the majority. Such a conclusion has immensely important implications for our thinking about organizations and about innovation in particular.

In an early social psychology study, people were shown blue and green slides and asked to categorize them accordingly. Those in an experimental group were exposed to a minority who consistently categorized some of the blue slides as green. This procedure, not surprisingly, had no impact on the majority correctly categorizing the blue slides. However, when people were subsequently asked to individually rate ambiguous 'blue-green' slides as either blue or green, over half rated the slides in a direction which was consistent with their having been influenced by the minority. A group not exposed to the minority showed no such effects. Similar influences have been demonstrated in studies of jury decision-making.

Research on minority influence suggests that 'conversion' is most likely to occur where the minority is consistent and confident in the presentation of arguments. Moreover, it is a behavioural style of persistence which is most likely to lead to attitude change and innovation. The prices of minority influence strategies, according to researchers, are unpopularity and conflict. As mentioned earlier, it is argued that innovation inevitably produces conflict, since it represents a challenge to the status quo. Again, research provides support for Machiavelli's views.

Work in this area also suggests that minority influence leads to more independence and to divergent and creative thinking. In another study, people were exposed to a minority which consistently judged blue stimuli as green. When these people were subsequently placed in a situation where a majority consistently and incorrectly rated red stimuli as orange, they showed almost complete independence and did not differ significantly from control subjects who made their judgements of the red stimuli alone. Those not exposed to minority dissent agreed with the majority's incorrect judgement of orange on over 70 per cent of trials.

In another study of originality, people were told that a majority or a minority had seen blue slides as green in previous studies. Each person was subsequently exposed to a single confederate of the experimenter who consistently rated blue slides as green. Finally, each subject was asked to respond seven times in a word association exercise to the words 'blue' or 'green'. Those exposed to a minority judgement gave more word associations and with a higher degree of originality than those exposed to a majority view. In reviewing this research, Charlan Nemeth (1989) concludes that:

> *...This work argues for the importance of minority dissent. Even dissent that is wrong. Further we assume that its import lies not in the truth of its position, or even in the likelihood that it will prevail. Rather it appears to stimulate divergent thoughts. Issues and problems are considered from more perspectives and, on balance,* [people] *detect new solutions and find more correct answers.*

What are the implications of this work for our understanding of innovation in work settings? First, minority influence provides an understanding of intra-group processes leading to creativity and innovation. Second, the theory suggests what the key processes involved in innovation in organizations are – *conflict* and *conversion* – while alerting us to the fact that unitary views of innovation (all innovation is good and is good for all in the organization) are overly simplistic. Third, it suggests the importance of dissent within organizations for independence and creativity. Fourth, it implies that individuals in small groups can bring about change in organizational settings through consistency, persistence and confidence, despite widespread beliefs in the immutability of large organizations. We not only should tolerate but should *encourage* minorities in organizations if diversity of views is to provide the seedbeds for innovation and creativity.

By drawing upon this research, an innovation implementation strategy can be developed. From this perspective, the responsibility for introducing an innovation can be vested in an overall project team who develop a clear vision of the innovation, take the initiative and persistently communicate and agitate to ensure implementation plans are successfully carried through. In order to succeed, the strategy depends on the commitment of a highly motivated (and ideally relatively senior) team. The group acts to influence the views and orientations of significant others towards the innovation they are attempting to implement. Six key elements are required:

i. The minority influence team must have a *clear vision* of what it intends to accomplish. This vision should be coherent and have the commitment of all team members.

ii. The team should be a small but powerful and *effective group* of individuals within the organization, ideally no more than about eight to ten people in size.

iii. The group must have a *clear message* about the potential values and benefits of introducing the change into the organization. This message should be worked out and rehearsed in advance to ensure consistency and communication.

iv. The group will need to *present its message persistently* and repeat-edly over a long period of time. It must develop, in consultation with other organization members, the strategy for implementation of the innovation.

v. The group must be prepared to *listen flexibly* and to respond posi-tively to the suggestions of those within the organization about inno-vation, but without diluting its intent to bring about a comprehensive change.

vi. The group must use *consultation* processes and involve, wherever possible, other organizational members in order to anticipate and deal with potential conflicts arising from the initiative.

Exercise 18 shows the steps involved in developing a clear minority influence strategy.

❏ Case Study : Minority Influence
In a Yorkshire primary health care team, the nurses (health visitors, district nurses, practice nurses, midwives) wanted to introduce telephone triage for one day a week – advising and categorizing patients requesting home visits from the general practitioners (GPs) and nurses. The GPs resisted this inno-vation, which they saw as inappropriately involving nursing staff in what had always been GP diagnostic activities. The nurses persistently pressed their proposals, since they saw the advantages to patients, GPs and their own job enrichment. Considerable conflict was generated as a consequence, culminating in a tense meeting at which the GPs ended arguing amongst themselves. Ten days after the meeting, the GPs held a further discussion amongst themselves and agreed to the nurses' proposals. Moreover, they insisted the new triage system be implemented on three days rather than one day a week (perhaps in the expectation it would fail). Within one month, home visits by GPs had decreased by 70 per cent and patients were reporting high levels of satisfaction with the nurses' visits and the telephone triage system in general. Eventually, the conflict generated by the innovation process declined, and all parties claimed responsibility for the success of the innovation! The nurses had persisted in the face of conflict and introduced an innovation which enriched their jobs, improved patient care and reduced GP involvement in unnecessary home visits. They had begun with a vision of how to improve patient care, supported each other as a minority influence group, and succeeded in implementing the innovation, even though they were in a power minority.

DEVELOPING A MINORITY INFLUENCE STRATEGY

EXERCISE 18

1.   What one area or practice or approach within your organization do you wish, ideally, you could change? Describe your vision of this change in a sentence or two.

2.   Who else could you inspire to work with you to bring about this change? Identify a small team of committed colleagues who would join with you and support each other in the change process.

3.   What would be the three main elements of the message you would want to send out to others in the organization to persuade them of the value of the change?

4.   What powerful others in your organization might be persuaded to support you?

5.   How could you most effectively get your message repeatedly heard by people within the organization to ensure that the process of educating and persuading them is ongoing and maintained?

6.   How could you arrange to get to hear the views of others in the organization in relation to the issues you are addressing?

7.   What obstacles are you most likely to meet, and, using your creative inspiration, how might you overcome and avoid them repeatedly?

8.   How could you encourage the participation of all those in the organization likely to be affected by the change – how can you meet with them, share information and encourage them to become involved in effectively managing the change process?

9.   How can you best prepare yourself to cope with conflict and unpopularity?

10. In a year's time or five years' time what do you hope to have achieved in relation to the change?

Respond to each of these ten questions and develop a plan for effectively implementing the change. Present your plan briefly to a supportive group and discuss how you could improve your strategy.

PARTICIPATIVE STRATEGY

Where there is general acceptance of the need for, and the value of, the innovation, a participative strategy can be employed. This is particularly appropriate where there is sufficient time available to go through a participation process. Participation involves three elements; interacting with people likely to be affected by the innovation; sharing information with them; and involving them in decision-making. Somewhat different from participative processes are consultation processes, where organizational members are simply consulted, but without having any real influence over decision-making. True participation involves all three elements – interacting with those affected by the innovation, giving them influence over decision-making and sharing information in both directions. A considerable amount of research has shown that resistance to innovation is reduced when people are involved in the innovation process.

Taking the example of introducing team-based working, a participative strategy could be employed where a good basis of team working already exists within an organization. First, an organizational map is drawn showing the locations of current team working. This enables the identification of potential areas from which team-based working can be spread. Organizational members who are already involved in team working can be included with those who are not in discussions to identify the broadest range of team locations and types. Those teams which already exist can be encouraged to review their effectiveness and advise on ways of changing team processes and structures to improve team performance generally throughout the organization. Organization support structures could also be reviewed by existing team members, to assess their contribution to the achievement of effective team-based working. It is valuable to involve those who are already committed to team working, since they can provide examples of good practice and act as ambassadors for the introduction of team-based working in the wider organization. The principle underlying this strategy is that interacting with (preferably face-to-face), sharing information with, and involving in decision-making, those likely to be affected by the innovation, is the most potent way of reducing resistance while shaping the innovation most effectively to meet the organizational needs.

POWER COERCIVE STRATEGY

When an innovation is likely to be resisted by a large group within the organization or there is simply insufficient time to engage in consultation or participation processes, some managers choose 'power coercive' strategies. These strategies can only be used by those with sufficient power in an organization to force the implementation of the innovation. The consequence of using power coercive strategies is that considerable animosity is generated amongst organizational members. In effect, organization members are forced by senior managers to accept the change against their judgement or will, often at the price of job security. Indeed, in many instances, power coercive strategies are the only way of bringing about unpopular changes. 'Downsizing' – reducing the number of employees in an organization – is obviously likely to generate huge resistance and consultation and participation processes are ineffective. Culture change programmes also often demand a huge degree of power-coercion to overcome the resistance to change which those immersed in 'old-culture' often manifest. For example, middle managers often strenuously resist the introduction of team-based working , despite its obvious advantages, because they correctly perceive that their management power and control will be curtailed as a consequence. In many organizations, power-coercion is employed as the principal strategy in bringing about change, but the cost of such approaches is that employees may see a mismatch between management talk of employee involvement, commitment and participation, and management practices of forcing through unpopular changes.

ECLECTIC STRATEGY

Richard Daft (1992) suggests combining a variety of methods to develop a strategy for implementing innovation. His approach involves seven techniques for changing implementation.

i. *Diagnose a true need for change.* As indicated earlier in this book, correctly identifying the nature of the problem is fundamental to effective innovation. It is therefore important to spend sufficient time diagnosing the true need for change and correctly identifying the nature of the problem. Many innovations fail simply because the wrong problem is identified.

ii. *Find an idea that fits the need.* This means making sure that the correct match is found between the nature of the problem and the innovation idea which is generated or discovered.

iii. *Get top management support.* Innovation attempts are more successful to the extent that people with power and seniority support the change.

iv. *Design the change for incremental implementation.* Daft argues that the prospects for success for innovations are improved dramatically if each part of the process can be designed and implemented sequentially. Then so called 'teething problems' can be managed one by one as they appear, rather than trying to deal with a whole jaw-full of problems at the same time.

v. *Develop plans to overcome resistance to change.* Align innovation plans with the needs and goals of users. Here it is important to ensure that the innovation meets a real need. If people within the organization do not believe that an innovation has value, or if top management does not support it, the organization will resist the change. The process of overcoming resistance to change therefore requires that the innovation actually meets the needs of those who are going to use or be affected by it. Other ways of reducing resistance include:

- *Communication and education.* Clear and persistent communication about the nature of the need, the value of the innovation and the process of implementation is likely to reduce resistance to change. Daft rightly argues that far more communication and education than managers think is necessary should be undertaken, since typically the amount required is underestimated.
- *Participation and involvement.* Extensive and early participation of those affected by the innovation is required in order to reduce resistance to change. As indicated above, participation in the innovation process is the single most potent way of reducing resistance.
- *Forcing and coercion.* Management power is used to overcome resistance by forcing employees to adopt the innovation. This approach should be used when time is of the essence and strong resistance is expected. Managers also have to consider the long term impacts of using such strategies.

(vi) *Create change teams.* Organizational innovations are implemented more successfully if innovation teams are created which carry responsibility for the successful implementation of the innovation.

(vii) *Foster idea champions.* Innovation champions are volunteers who are deeply committed to a particular innovation. They have the responsibility of ensuring that all technical supports are available and they persuade people about the value of the implementation.

Dart's seven elements of an eclectic strategy can be used collectively to ensure the success of innovation attempts. Consideration of them indicates two important themes: the need to consider the reactions of all those affected by the innovation, and the value of organizational agents who explicitly support innovation. We will now consider two mechanisms by which these issues can be addressed – *Forcefield/ Stakeholder Analysis* and the creation of an *Office of Innovation*.

FORCEFIELD AND STAKEHOLDER ANALYSIS

Exercise 19 describes a strategy for reducing resistance to innovation, based on a combination of stakeholder and forcefield analysis. This exercise enables the development of an overview of how much resistance to innovation is likely to be present and where major problems may arise. It enables strategy planning for managing resistance to change and participation processes within an organization. It can be helpful to work through this process with several colleagues, as comparing the resulting forcefields may produce valuable and useful insights into the current organizational situation. The forcefield analysis model was developed by Kurt Lewin (1935) who described all situations in which we find ourselves as a 'temporary equilibrium held in place by two sets of forces: driving forces which push change along and restraining forces which pull back against change'. Understanding those forces will help the innovator towards successful implementation.

THE OFFICE OF INNOVATION

In the late 1970s, the Eastman Kodak Company developed the 'Office of Innovation' model to help facilitate innovation. This type of model has been implemented by many other organizations, including AMOCO, Atomic Energy of Canada, Bell Canada, North Western Bell and Union Carbide. The system is aimed at bringing together those involved in the innovation process in order to ensure success, and involves five stages.

1.   Idea generation
The originator of the idea meets with a volunteer facilitator in the Office of Innovation and explains the idea in outline form. The Office of Innovation is usually virtual and does not exist as a formal

ANALYSING AND MANAGING RESISTANCE TO INNOVATION

EXERCISE 19

Step 1: define the innovation you wish to implement. The outcome of the innovation will be the equilibrium which you are hoping to achieve in the future. It is therefore important that this outcome is clearly defined.

Step 2: now identify all those individuals and groups who could have an influence on your ability to introduce the innovation into your organization. For each of these 'stakeholders', identify the major advantages and disadvantages which may accrue to them with the introduction of the innovation.

Stakeholder	Advantages	Disadvantages

Step 3: the forcefield. Draw a 'forcefield' with an arrow to represent each stakeholder. For each arrow in the forcefield you will need to decide:

(a) the direction of the arrow – although it is sometime difficult to know exactly how others are thinking, for the purposes of this exercise you must make a decision based on your current knowledge of the situation. If the arrow represents a group within which there are mixed opinions, you must still decide which side, on balance, the group as a whole will be. You may however indicate the situation within the arrow, for example by patchy shading.

(b) the size of the arrow – this will represent the relative power of the individual group or factor to influence the introduction of the innovation, either positively or negatively. You may wish to use colour and shading to make the arrows as representative of your view of the situation as possible.

Restraining Forces

↓   ↓   ↓   ↓   ↓

———— INTRODUCTION OF INNOVATION ————

⇧   ⇧   ⇧   ⇧   ⇧   ⇧   ⇧

Driving Forces

continued

continued

Step 4: action planning. After contemplating the forcefield that you have drawn, you may have some new insights into the situation. Does the environment for the introduction of the innovation look more positive than you had thought? Alternatively, are the arrows more heavily weighted on the restraining side of the innovation line? This is a good point at which to consider the feasibility of achieving this particular innovation at this time. With some rebalancing the environment may well be able to support the proposed innovation. In which case, a review of the forcefield will enable you to decide where you need to exert energy in order to:

(a) decrease the power and influence of the restraining forces;
(b) increase the power and influence of the driving forces.

Based on the analysis, what actions could you take to reduce the influence of the restraining forces and increase the power of the supporting forces? Your action plan should be helpful in determining strategies for moving forward. Try to identify ways in which the balance of the forces could be weighted more strongly in your favour. This may be by finding new helping forces, or by trying to eliminate or lessen the effect of some of the hindering forces. People often find that it tends to be easier to do the latter. To use the car analogy, it is as if one's foot is already down on the floor and there is no way to increase the driving force. The easiest solution may well be to take off the handbrake!

- Action plans are best **written** down. The action of writing them helps to clarify the issues and to highlight any problem areas.

- Once the innovation has been identified and an overall plan has been developed, it is useful to break it down into smaller **specific action points.** The more specific they are, the easier it is to plan and monitor progress.

- Actions should be **measurable.** What outcomes are anticipated that will signify that the actions have been successfully completed? If a number of outcomes are identified, representing stages in the process of the implementation of the innovation, it may be that required action can be broken down into still more specific actions.

- Action plans must be **realistic.** Innovations often fail because unachievable goals are set.

- Action plans and outcomes should have a clear **timescale** attached to them.

continued _

Step 4: action planning. After contemplating the forcefield that you have drawn, you may have some new insights into the situation. Does the environment for the introduction of the innovation look more positive than you had thought? Alternatively, are the arrows more heavily weighted on the restraining side of the innovation line? This is a good point at which to consider the feasibility of achieving this particular innovation at this time. With some rebalancing the environment may well be able to support the proposed innovation. In which case, a review of the forcefield will enable you to decide where you need to exert energy in order to:

(a) decrease the power and influence of the restraining forces;
(b) increase the power and influence of the driving forces.

Based on the analysis, what actions could you take to reduce the influence of the restraining forces and increase the power of the supporting forces? Your action plan should be helpful in determining strategies for moving forward. Try to identify ways in which the balance of the forces could be weighted more strongly in your favour. This may be by finding new helping forces, or by trying to eliminate or lessen the effect of some of the hindering forces. People often find that it tends to be easier to do the latter. To use the car analogy, it is as if one's foot is already down on the floor and there is no way to increase the driving force. The easiest solution may well be to take off the handbrake!

- Action plans are best **written** down. The action of writing them helps to clarify the issues and to highlight any problem areas.

- Once the innovation has been identified and an overall plan has been developed, it is useful to break it down into smaller **specific action points.** The more specific they are, the easier it is to plan and monitor progress.

- Actions should be **measurable.** What outcomes are anticipated that will signify that the actions have been successfully completed? If a number of outcomes are identified, representing stages in the process of the implementation of the innovation, it may be that required action can be broken down into still more specific actions.

- Action plans must be **realistic.** Innovations often fail because unachievable goals are set.

- Action plans and outcomes should have a clear **timescale** attached to them.

ANALYSING AND MANAGING RESISTANCE TO INNOVATION

EXERCISE 19

Step 1: define the innovation you wish to implement. The outcome of the innovation will be the equilibrium which you are hoping to achieve in the future. It is therefore important that this outcome is clearly defined.

Step 2: now identify all those individuals and groups who could have an influence on your ability to introduce the innovation into your organization. For each of these 'stakeholders', identify the major advantages and disadvantages which may accrue to them with the introduction of the innovation.

Stakeholder	Advantages	Disadvantages
_____	_____	_____
_____	_____	_____
_____	_____	_____
_____	_____	_____
_____	_____	_____
_____	_____	_____

Step 3: the forcefield. Draw a 'forcefield' with an arrow to represent each stakeholder. For each arrow in the forcefield you will need to decide:

(a) the direction of the arrow – although it is sometime difficult to know exactly how others are thinking, for the purposes of this exercise you must make a decision based on your current knowledge of the situation. If the arrow represents a group within which there are mixed opinions, you must still decide which side, on balance, the group as a whole will be. You may however indicate the situation within the arrow, for example by patchy shading.

(b) the size of the arrow – this will represent the relative power of the individual group or factor to influence the introduction of the innovation, either positively or negatively. You may wish to use colour and shading to make the arrows as representative of your view of the situation as possible.

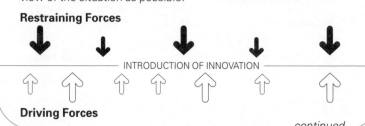

Restraining Forces

INTRODUCTION OF INNOVATION

Driving Forces

continued

building space, but may be managed by a small number of individuals throughout the organization. The facilitator's role is to explore the idea, the technical and resource implications, and to act as a guide and supporter to the idea originator. The facilitator helps to guide the originator and the idea through the corporate labyrinth and in the acquisition of resources to support the innovation.

2.　Initial screening
If, as the result of initial meetings between the facilitator and the originator, the idea is to be taken forward, the originator prepares a one-or two-page project proposal. The facilitator and originator jointly select a group of experts within the organization to review the idea, usually referred to as 'consultants'. Between five and fifteen consultants are chosen. They are asked to review the proposal and to comment in terms of novelty, market needs, technological feasibility, improvements and whether they wish to continue to be involved in the process.

3.　Group review
The consultants' reviews are collated and a meeting is held between the facilitator and the idea originator. If the originator determines to go ahead, a group review meeting is held at which the consultants, the originator and the facilitator meet together in one or more of a series of meetings to assess the support of the consultants for the idea and decide if and how to proceed.

4.　Seeking sponsorship
As the idea is explored in more detail, its true worth as an innovation becomes clear and if the decision is made to proceed, sponsorship is sought. Here the major concern is to identify an innovation champion within the organization who will sponsor (or elicit sponsorship for) the development of the innovation.

5.　Sponsorship
The final stage is the more formal stage where sponsorship is actually achieved and the innovation begins to be developed and implemented within the organizational setting.

Kodak report that, as a result of this process, between 40 per cent and 60 per cent of ideas are lost during the first two stages and that only 9 per cent are finally firmly sponsored and funded for development. The Office of Innovation provides a means by which those with ideas can find support in the form of facilitators and consultants who will help them develop the idea and guide it through the various difficult stages of implementation within the organization. This ensures that innovations generated from the bottom of the organization have a good chance of success. Eastman Kodak estimate that the value of ideas harvested in one year alone from the Office of Innovation project was approximately 300 million dollars, while the cost of the process was only 0.3 per cent of the potential revenue.

THE PHILOSOPHY OF THE OFFICE OF INNOVATION

- Ideas and people are fragile.

- Ideas and people need to be nurtured.

- All ideas should be given a hearing.

- The originator of an idea needs assistance in developing the idea and in promoting it in the organization.

- The originator is the initial advocate of an idea and should be actively involved in its development.

- Only ideas which have been developed, assessed and convincingly demonstrate potential value will be brought to management. Both marketing and technical issues need to be addressed in the development of an idea.

- Employees benefit from the opportunity to interact with other professionals from different perspectives.

- A mediator is often necessary to facilitate the communication of people from different cultures and who may possess clashing personalities.

- The most effective way to proceed is not necessarily the most efficient.

(Adapted from Rosenfeld and Servo, 1990.)

CHAPTER SUMMARY

Managing innovation begins with carefully analysing the problem and clarifying a vision for change. The successful innovator (whether individual or group) must then plan every stage in the innovation process and select change strategies most suitable to that stage, the organizational context and to the vision itself. Implementing a change towards greater employee involvement by using only power-coercive strategies is sure to undermine the process. Ideally, there will be an integration and consistency between the content, context and the process of the innovation.

Innovation is a long path paved with conflict requiring a vision of change, courage in the face of conflict, persistence in the face of resistance, and the wisdom to steer a course through the complex currents of change from the beginning to the end of the process. The great innovators of society – Galileo, Martin Luther King, Aung San Suu Kyi, the Greens, Darwin, the Feminists – all had to maintain a vision, show courage, wisdom and determination in order to make progress. The same is true for the person who wishes to bring about change for the better in the world of work.

Chapter Seven

Key Innovations

Good ideas are shot down by people who assume the future is merely an extension of the past, (that) the ideas that have brought us to where we are today are the same ideas that are going to take us to tomorrow.
Joel A. Barker

Faced with the choice between changing one's mind and proving that there is no need to do so, almost everybody gets busy on the proof.
John Kenneth Galbraith

As organizations enter the third millennium there is a recognition in all sectors – private, public and voluntary – that in order to develop and grow effectively in the context of vigorous competition for limited resources and markets, innovation and creativity are essential. But in what areas should organizations initially make major changes? Before addressing this question, two aspects of the innovation landscape are worth highlighting. The first is that there is a clear separation between the rhetoric of innovation and the reality of what is happening within organizations. The second is that many managers seem unaware of the need for a multi-component approach to stimulating effective innovation.

RHETORIC VERSUS REALITY

From research in manufacturing organizations, my colleagues and I have found that human resource management is generally not emphasized in these organizations. Forty per cent of the 120 firms we work with have no specialist personnel staff, whilst two thirds have no formal personnel or HRM strategy. Almost half of the companies have no written training strategy, despite widespread attempts to train in areas such as quality. Training needs analysis is also poor or absent in over half of the companies. The skill requirements and responsibilities of shop floor jobs remain limited for many workers; most jobs are repetitive and monotonous. Two thirds of firms have no deliberate policy of job rotation. Equal opportunities is not generally perceived as an important issue, with two thirds of firms having no stated policy in this area (West *et al.*,1995). Moreover, analysis of innovation within these organizations indicates that innovation is surprisingly infrequent.

Within the British National Health Service (NHS) there is a similar low level of innovation in areas such as human resource management and training (West and Anderson, 1992). This is despite the fact that the NHS employs more than one million employees and has an overall budget many times the size of most large organizations in Europe. Even within major commercial organizations there are indications that the management of human resources and other critical aspects of organizational functioning is remarkably primitive, with organizational commitment declining as a consequence of poor people management and high levels of job insecurity. Many, perhaps most, organizations are 50 years behind what organizational scientists and management gurus are discussing. Journals such as *The Harvard Business Review* and management schools such as INSEAD (the famous French management school) and the London Business School are often exploring ideas and concepts which are considerable travelling distances from the stations at which most organizations are waiting. Despite the rhetoric of many management books, there is truly a lot more being said than being done. While most managers clearly understand much of the rhetoric of management theory, many of them are failing to implement it in practice.

THE NEED FOR A MULTI-COMPONENT STRATEGY

There is persuasive research evidence that organizations intent on introducing innovation and change are more successful to the extent that they implement a number of elements of the change process concurrently, and that teamwork is a particularly important element (Macy and Izumi, 1993). But when organizations face such a vast array of potential changes, where do they begin? There is a torrent of acronyms associated with organizational innovation, such as BPR (Business Process Re-engineering), TQM (Total Quality Management), PRP (Performance-Related Pay), AMT (Advanced Manufacturing Technology), JIT (Just-in-Time Inventory Control), PDP (Personal Development Planning) and so on. Deciding which approaches to follow can seem like simply picking fads and fashions from business school fashion magazines with consequent major difficulties in implementation.

I believe there are four central themes and related priority practices which should be pursued if organizations are to effectively implement innovation:

First, organizations need clear *vision and direction* which act both to motivate energy amongst the people within the organization as well as enabling the derivation of clear goals for departments, teams and individuals. With a clear and inspiring vision of the content of the future and the process of arriving there, organizational forces are invigorated and directed towards change.

Second, a high level of *participation and involvement* is essential if the skills, energy and knowledge of those working in the organization are to be used most effectively and in ways which enhance well being. This requires the commitment of people with diverse views, and constructive processes of conflict and controversy as their differing perspectives are reconciled in creative outcomes.

Third is a commitment to excellence in task performance – *task orientation*. A concern with quality in all areas of functioning, critical self-appraisal, debate, analysis and vigorous but constructive questioning are hallmarks of innovative organizations. Mechanisms must be found which facilitate inter-professional, cross-departmental, and integrated working and task focus within organizations which foster constructive debate and questioning.

Finally, and most obviously is the importance of *support for innovation*. The commitment to a strategy of innovation is essential if organizations are truly to foster innovation and encourage creativity in organizations. But this means support in practice, not only in principle.

Following is a description of four key areas of innovation with practical illustrations of how these issues can be addressed in organizations.

GOAL-SETTING AND FEEDBACK

A consistent finding to emerge from research in industrial/organizational psychology over the last 100 years, is that setting clear objectives for people at work and providing them with frequent, largely positive and accurate feedback is a powerful way of improving performance. The introduction of appraisals, performance-related pay, performance management, management by objectives, and stretch objectives has occurred in response to a recognition of the importance of goal-setting and feedback. However, the implementation of these approaches has often created new problems rather than solving old ones. Performance appraisals, for example, often involve meetings between a manager and a member of staff in which previous performance is reviewed, goals are set for the future, career development is explored and pay and bonus issues are decided as well. This can be likened to mixing up the soup, the main course, the dessert and the coffee all on one plate and then stirring in the napkin for good measure as well. Research suggests that the principal effective element of the appraisal process is collaboratively setting goals for future individual performance. Feedback should not be delayed until an annual meeting, but should be built in to the individual's job and occur on a day-to-day basis. People learn better when they receive feedback as soon as possible after completing a task and if that feedback is accurate in giving them information about deficits and successes in performance.

But if performance targets are not set collaboratively and wisely, they can lead to unanticipated difficulties. In the implementation of performance targets in the university sector, university departments are rated every three years on the basis of publications by members of the departments. This has led to universities hiring people around the time of the assessment exercises in order that they can win additional funding as a consequence of getting improved ratings, rather like transfer deals in football clubs. The effects on the climates of the departments seem rather damaging; those departments which do well show an improvement in organizational climate and particularly in support for innovation, while those which do badly show a continual decline. Thus vicious or virtual cycles are set in motion as a consequence of performance measurement systems, which academics themselves have often not been involved in determining. Our research, at the Institute of Work Psychology, has revealed other examples in which work teams have performance targets imposed on them, which team members do not value and consequently bypass. Human ingenuity finds its expression often in ways of suggesting to senior management that targets are being reached, when close examination reveals that they are not. When performance is measured, people change their behaviour, but not always in predictable ways. Introducing innovations which improve goal-setting should therefore involve those who have to meet the goals in the process of setting them. Goal setting in conjunction with the individuals, teams or departments which have to achieve them can be a powerful means for improving performance.

The first step in the process is to determine the direction key actors in the organization wish to take. Where should the organization be in ten years' time? The mission of the organization must also be articulated – what are we here for? What is it we are trying to achieve? Answers to these questions lead to the unfolding of associated objectives and strategies for achieving them (a possible statement of vision, mission and objectives is shown in the boxed example on p. 125).

From a statement of vision, mission and objectives, the objectives of departments, units and teams can be derived in close consultation with their members. And from there, in turn, can come the objectives for individuals in the organization. Visions, clear direction, goals, objectives and performance feedback are vital for all aspects of organizational functioning, and for innovation efforts to be appropriately directed. Such visions, clear direction and goals must be effectively and persistently communicated to all in the organization.

WOMEN AT WORK

One of the key challenges for organizations is to learn to manage and harness the diversity of perspectives in modern heterogeneous organizations in ways which stimulate creativity and innovation. Diversity in the workforce leads to diversity of views, attitudes, skills, ideas, assumptions and paradigms. While it may be uncomfortable initially to manage the consequent disagreements, such diversity is the root of creativity and innovation. Diversity in the workforce includes variation in gender, cultural background, ethnicity, age, professional backgrounds, educational backgrounds and values. The second priority we address is ensuring participation in the workplace and the problems in this area are exemplified best by the experience of women at work.

One phenomenon in the workplace which is striking above all to an organizational scientist is the hierarchical status gradient in

INSTITUTE OF WORK PSYCHOLOGY

VISION, MISSION AND OBJECTIVES

Vision

The Institute of Work Psychology is, within ten years, a leading world research institute examining issues of effectiveness and well-being at work. It is widely acknowledged among colleagues in psychology and related disciplines as a centre of excellence and as a leading exponent of influential theoretical positions in this area. The Institute is also a model for the management of research institutes within the area. The staff of the Institute represent amongst the most able researchers internationally. Members of the Institute are proud of their affiliation and acknowledge the excellence with which the Institute is managed as a research centre.

Mission

- To significantly advance understanding about the effectiveness of people, groups and organizations at work, and to discover clear communicable evidence about effectiveness at work.

- To attract and support excellent scholars in the field, nationally and internationally in order to develop theory and research which is of the highest quality, innovative and widely influential.

- To influence practice in organizations in all sectors.

- To develop interventions, tools and techniques which promote effectiveness at work.

- To be a model for the management of research centres.

Objectives

- To develop theory which has international influence, generating further theoretical development and research.

- To make important discoveries about effectiveness and well-being of people at work and to communicate these discoveries widely.

- To influence research and practice nationally and internationally in the area of psychology of work and thereby to be able to point annually to four international publications which draw centrally upon the work of those in the Institute.

continued

continued

- To provide practical support and stimulation for scholars of international repute to study at the Institute and to secure sufficient funding to enable this. To this end to attract at least two senior researchers from overseas each year, for minimum stays of three months.

- To demonstrate best practices in how workplaces can be managed in ways which ensure effectiveness, well-being, commitment and growth and development of all staff. To draw upon best practices in R & D organizations in other sectors to develop effective management practices and styles.

- To demonstrate real influence on organizational practice and added practical value for organizations which take up the findings disseminated by the Institute or utilize the tools developed. To this end to demonstrate substantial cost savings or increased effectiveness in organizations which utilize the findings of the Institute.

- To produce increasing numbers of publications per year in top international journals such as *Administrative Science Quarterly, Journal of Applied Psychology, Psychological Bulletin, Academy of Management Journal, Academy of Management Review, Personnel Psychology.*

- To produce, every two years, a publication describing the range of interventions, tools and techniques produced within the Unit, and to set and achieve annual targets for their implementation in predetermined numbers of organizations.

- To produce increasing numbers of publications in top practitioner outlets per year, such as *The Financial Times, The Economist, The Harvard Business Review, Management Today, The European.*

- To produce two or three books in every five-year period, which are acknowledged as highly influential in our field.

- Each member of the Institute, all other things being equal, to produce two to three good quality journal articles and at least one practitioner article each year.

- To influence public policy in relation to work place practices and to be able to demonstrate this influence over any five-year period.

favour of men. For example, my colleagues have interviewed more than 400 senior managers in manufacturing organizations in the United Kingdom. We have only interviewed one woman manager and she was married to the managing director of the company. Gender segregation is also rife. Secretaries throughout organizations are predominantly women, nurses are predominantly women; doctors have been traditionally, and still are, predominantly men. Of the one million managers at middle and senior level in Britain, only four per cent are women. In the US, long considered as the vanguard of equal opportunities action, only five per cent of senior executive positions are occupied by women, and this figure has barely changed in the last ten years. The same is true in the university sector. Oxford University has 361 professors, 20 of whom are women (*The Times*, 8th July 1996). Barriers to women's advancement include gender stereotyping, the education system, attitudinal barriers, stress at work and home–work conflicts.

There is much rhetoric about equal opportunities within organizations, but in reality change is agonisingly slow. Even when change does occur, there are still many invisible obstacles which undermine the position of women. In our studies of National Health Service managers and doctors, many of whom are women, we have found that stress levels associated with occupying a non-stereotypical gender role are extremely high. Apparently, the invisible obstacles to women who occupy traditionally male roles cause pain and damage to women at work. Yet women managers occupying positions equivalent to those of men managers in organizations are, on average, better educated.

Research suggests that women managers are motivated by characteristics which are particularly valuable to organizations concerned to initiate innovation. Women tend to be more motivated by their needs for growth and development, finding new and improved ways of working, doing jobs in their own creative way, contributing to society, and fitting their work life in with life outside. Male managers, on the other hand, tend to be motivated more by security, pay, fringe benefits and promotion (Nicholson and West, 1988). These latter orientations, of course, are much more difficult to satisfy in modern organizations where contractual insecurity and promotional opportunities are limited. This profile of women managers' orientations suggests they have much which is unique to contribute to innovation, yet the structural and attitudinal barriers in their way considerably blunt their contribution.

There is some suggestion from research that women's style of leadership in organizations may be more suited to the organizations of the future. They tend to adopt a more 'transformational' style of leadership inspiring those with whom they work, encouraging, reassuring and building relationships with them. Men, in contrast, tend to adopt a more 'transactional' style, rewarding and punishing behaviours which they respectively seek to encourage or reduce. Women's leadership style therefore appears well suited to fostering innovation since it encourages intrinsic rather than extrinsic orientations to work.

In short, research suggests that women have much to offer organizations of the future in developing innovation and that (quite apart from the moral and ethical issues raised) there is an enormous waste of resources, both to organizations and to society in general, as long as women continue to be excluded from full participation in the workplace.

The Hansard Society Commission has recommended the following innovations in organizations, to meet the challenge of gender discrimination in the workplace:

- A fully developed and regularly reviewed equal opportunities policy.
- Equal opportunities training for all involved in selection and promotion decisions.
- Dual interviewing – both men and women interviewing prospective job or promotion candidates.
- Precise job specifications so that fairer selection and promotion decisions are made.
- Objective assessment criteria for selection and promotion.
- External advertising.
- Equal opportunity audits.
- Monitoring of equal opportunity issues in selection and promotion.
- Clear targets for balanced gender representation.
- Senior level part-time/job sharing arrangements.
- Flexi-time.
- Working at home.
- Annual hours rather than weekly hours of work (enables greater flexibility).
- Mobility requirements dropped or modified since they discriminate against women and people with families.
- Dual career job search to meet the career needs of both partners.
- Age limit requirements dropped.

- Career break schemes.
- Nurseries in the workplace.
- Childcare vouchers.
- Parental leave.
- Enhanced maternity leave.
- Other childcare help.
- Internal promotion policies.
- Equal opportunity advertising.
- Women-only training courses.
- Boardroom commitment to change.
- Awareness training for all staff.

Managerial vision, commitment and courage are required to ensure that such innovations are implemented effectively since resistance is inevitable. The strategic as well as moral imperatives of these changes are nevertheless compelling.

TEAMWORK IN ORGANIZATIONS

A third major way in which innovation can be encouraged is through the introduction of team-based organization. In the US for example, over 80 per cent of organizations with more than 100 employees now use teams in some way, and many British organizations are trying to follow this lead. However, there is much rhetoric about the introduction of teamwork, but the reality is rather different. In many organizations, managers appear quite unsure about how to introduce in practice team-based working (Mohrman, Cohen and Mohrman, 1995). Our research in the National Health Service has revealed that despite the enormous size of the organization and the clear need for a team-based approach, there is relatively little effective team-based working. Indeed, discovering team-based working outside of management teams, community mental health teams, and some primary health care teams, is like searching for opals in the desert. They are there but rare, and it takes a lot of searching. Issues of effective teamworking have been addressed in another book in this series (West, 1994). Here what is argued is that teamworking is an important area of innovation which can improve organizational effectiveness and innovativeness, by bringing together people with diverse perspectives and professional backgrounds. Teamworking also offers the opportunity of developing a wide range of ideas for new and improved ways of doing things at work.

Research by Macy and Izumi (1993) examined a large number of organizational change studies in order to determine their effectiveness. The results show that those interventions with the greatest effects on financially-related measures of organizational performance were team-related interventions. These also reduced turnover (employee departures) and absenteeism more than did other interventions, showing that team-oriented practices can have broad positive effects in organizations. Another analysis of surveys of organizational practices, as well as 185 case studies of innovation in management practices, found compelling evidence that teams contribute to improved organizational effectiveness, particularly increasing efficiency and quality. Other researchers provide evidence of the impact of team-based work practices in organizational performance. A study of over 700 work establishments found that those in which teamwork was developed were more effective in their performance than those in which teams were not used. Using team based working within organizations represents a major innovative initiative which can have profound systemic effects. Throughout this book, evidence has been offered of the impact of teamworking upon organizational innovation. Now the challenge is to build or restructure organizations which enable team-based working, rather than simply attempting to graft teams on to traditional structures (often unsuccessfully) (Mohrman, Cohen and Mohrman, 1995; Markiewicz and West, 1996).

Figure 5 shows the factors which must be considered when introducing team based-working and a four-stage model for implementation. The complexity of the process makes it clear that transitions to team-based organizations take a long time to occur; they are pervasive, involving almost all aspects of the organization; they involve the whole organization; and they require deep changes in the culture of the organization. They include empowering teams; the relinquishing of middle management's control; the end of rigid hierarchies; the development of lateral communication and integration across teams, departments and functions; and moving from cultures of individualism to cultures of collectivism (Mohrman *et al.*, 1995). Innovation indeed!

SUPPORT FOR INNOVATION

Many organizations expound support for innovation in their mission statements. However, boards and top management teams in

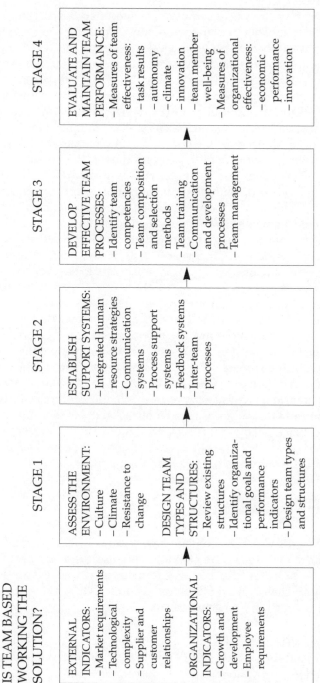

Figure 5: The Four Stage Model. (From Markiewicz and West, 1996.)

particular are notoriously conservative and often fail in practice to encourage innovation within their organizations. Although rhetoric is widespread, there is little practical support. However, there are good examples of organizational support for innovation. Some organizations (such as 3M) offer employees a substantial percentage of their time to exploit new ideas. Others encourage innovative ideas from people on the shop floor, urging them to champion ideas and implement them within the organization. The example of the innovative use of brush heads in the wire and cable company described in the first chapter of the book is a useful model. In one automotive parts company I visit, a secretary/clerk was given the job of co-ordinating all teamwork within the organization shortly after it was introduced. This was on the initiative and with the encouragement of a farsighted managing director who is committed to innovation, individual growth, development and risk-taking. This secretary/clerk grew in stature within a year or two and is giving talks on the management of teamworking in organizations to senior executives from all over the country.

Organizations must encourage and reward innovation at all levels, but encouragement and reward alone are insufficient. There must be a commitment to provide resources, time and co-operation in the development of new and improved ways of doing things, from wherever the ideas come within the organization (such as the Office of Innovation described in Chapter 6). That means committing energy, personal time and the necessary resources to those with the ideas for innovation and the enthusiasm and motivation to put them into practice. Organizational rhetoric in support of innovation swiftly becomes an inflated currency if it is not backed with gold. Described below are ten practical examples of organizational support for innovation.

SUPPORTING INNOVATION

REWARDS
United Electric Control Company has a 'valued-ideas' programme. One hundred US dollars are paid for every useable idea. Short-term groups (Action Centers) are also formed by employees to solve specific problems. Any employee can set up a Center at any time and conference rooms are constantly available.

BEST PRACTICE
PepsiCo send senior executives on field trips to observe companies renowned for innovation.

RESOURCES

Frito-Lay Inc. make 10,000 packages of snacks per minute and committees and researchers generate hundreds of new product ideas each year. These ideas are tested on 100 people each night, five nights a week, who sample up to 10 different products. Frito-Lay is an innovative company which devotes a substantial portion of its resources to innovation.

A LEARNING ORGANIZATION

Federal Express has a customer-service staff of 45,000 in 700 locations in 15 countries. In order to keep them abreast of the 1,700 changes to products and services which occur each year, interactive video units are installed in all locations. Twenty-five laser discs are updated with a CD-Rom every six weeks. The savings on travel expenses and the need for instructors amounts to tens of millions of dollars. Each employee takes a job knowledge test every six months after four hours of study time. The test provides a prescription for how areas of failure can be improved and workers who do not pass the test simply repeat the retraining via computer.

SWITCHING STRUCTURES

In order to innovate, organizations need to be organic at the ideas stage and mechanistic at the implementation stage. The Philips Corporation, which produces building materials, creates 150 teams once a year (five employees per team) to brainstorm and problem solve for a five-day period. After five days they revert to their normal organizational structure to implement the changes.

INNOVATIVE STRUCTURES

Illinois Tool Works forms a new division every time a new product is developed. Currently it has 90 product divisions and the organization is highly decentralized with each division controlling R & D, marketing and manufacturing. Closeness to customers is emphasized and employees spend as much time introducing innovation into how the factory works and jobs are organized as they do on new product development.

CONTINUOUS IMPROVEMENT PROGRAMMES (CIP)

These programmes are designed to harness employee knowledge to improve products, services and work practices. Using such systems,

Cadillac reduced warranty defects by 60 per cent in three years, moved from seventeenth place to fourth in the league table of customer satisfaction, and increased productivity by 50 per cent in three years. Elements of CIP include:

- A plan to improve all operations continuously;
- Benchmarking company strategic plans against the world's best;
- Close partnerships with suppliers and customers;
- A deep understanding of customers' needs;
- A focus on preventing, not just correcting, mistakes;
- A commitment to improving quality throughout the organization.

CREATIVE DEPARTMENTS

Raytheon has had a 'New Product Centre' in place for 20 years. The Centre gives staff autonomy to develop new ideas while building close working relationships with other departments. Some R & D and quality departments, suitably empowered, can fulfil a similar function; Raychem (UK) has a top level team specifically charged with developing creativity and innovation throughout the company.

VENTURE TEAMS

Dow Chemicals created a Venture Team that has total freedom to establish new venture projects for any department in the company. In large organizations such as IBM, new venture teams are like companies within a company and are used to free creative people from bureaucracy. IBM sets up one such company a year – IBM's personal computer was originally developed by a venture group.

IDEA CHAMPIONS

Texas Instruments reviewed its innovation attempts and discovered that those which failed had no champion who believed passionately in the idea and would fight to see it implemented. Now, only innovations with vigorous champions are supported. When Steven Wozniak tried to get Hewlett Packard to invest in his idea of connecting microcomputers to TV sets in 1975, they declined. Wozniac left the company and, along with Steven Jobs, formed a new company called Apple Computers.

But there is no one best way of supporting innovation. Importing practices from other companies and cultures can stimulate innovation in organizations, but if these practices are not appropriately aligned with the organization culture, they may well fail. There are various routes to encouraging innovation, each of which has its strengths and weaknesses. However, the four principles just articulated – clear vision and objectives; high levels of participation; commitment to excellence in task performance; and practical support for innovation – are central themes in any strategy for innovation.

CHAPTER SUMMARY

...a broad constituency for workplace change has emerged... during the last two decades. Employers seek to provide better-quality goods and services at lower costs, employees to save jobs and recover income loss, unions to rebuild their institutional strength, and governments to rebuild faith in public institutions. The central question is whether these diverse groups can collaborate in the creation of new systems of work that meet the needs of the various parties involved. (Applebaum and Batt, 1994.)

Innovation involves risk-taking and requires courage, but 'business as usual' no longer works. Organizations consequently must develop a deep reflexivity in their approaches to work. Reflexivity is the extent to which organizations, teams, departments and individuals reflect upon and challenge organizational objectives, strategies and processes and adapt them accordingly. Organizations and teams which practise reflexivity and are prepared to continually challenge and re-define their organizational roles, goals and paradigms, via processes of innovation, develop a more comprehensive and penetrating intellectual representation of their roles. They better anticipate and manage problems, and they deal with conflict as a valuable process asset within the organization, encouraging effectiveness, growth and development. The most reflexive organizations are those within which there is a maelstrom of activity, debate, argument, innovation and a real sense of involvement of all employees. Those in organizations must learn not simply to expand the rhetoric of innovation, but to act and 'just do it' in relation to best practice and innovation. Wise, thoughtful management of change will promote effective innovation, but we need organizational leaders who have the courage to implement the rhetoric they are convinced by rather than simply repeating it.

Whatever you intend to do, or dream you can, begin it. Boldness has genius, power and magic in it. Begin it now. Goethe

APPENDIX 1: EXTRACT FROM THE TEAM CLIMATE INVENTORY

Date: _____

Team: _____

Instructions

This questionnaire asks about the climate or atmosphere in your work group or team. It asks about how people tend to work together in your team, how frequently you interact, the team's aims and objectives, and how much practical support and assistance is given towards the implementation of new and improved ways of doing things. There is no 'right' or 'wrong' answer to any of the questions – it is more important that you give an accurate and honest response to each question. Do not spend too long on any one question. First reactions are usually best. For each question consider how your team tends in general to be or how you feel in general about the climate within your team. Please circle your chosen answers using a ball point pen.

Part I Communication and Innovation

	Strongly disagree	Disagree	Neither agree nor disagree	Agree	Strongly agree
6. In this team we take the time needed to develop new ideas.	1	2	3	4	5
8. Everyone's view is listened to, even if it is in a minority.	1	2	3	4	5
17. Members of the team provide and share resources to help in the application of new ideas.	1	2	3	4	5
21. People in this team are always searching for fresh, new ways of looking at problems.	1	2	3	4	5

continued

continued --

	Strongly disagree	Disagree	Neither agree nor disagree	Agree	Strongly agree
26. Members of the team meet frequently to talk both formally and informally.	1	2	3	4	5

Part II Objectives

	Not at all		Somewhat		Completely
27. How clear are you about what your team objectives are?	1	2	3	4	5
28. To what extent to you think they are useful and appropriate objectives?	1	2	3	4	5
34. How worthwhile do you think these objectives are to the organization?	1	2	3	4	5
37. To what extent do you think members of your team are committed to these objectives?	1	2	3	4	5

Part III Task Style

	To a very little extent		To some extent		To a very great extent
39. Do you and your colleagues monitor each other so as to maintain a higher standard of work?	1	2	3	4	5
41. Does the team critically appraise potential weaknesses in what it is doing in order to achieve the best possible outcome?	1	2	3	4	5
42. Do members of the team build on each other's ideas in order to achieve the best possible outcome?	1	2	3	4	5
44. Does the team have clear criteria which members try to meet in order to achieve excellence as a team?	1	2	3	4	5

REFERENCES

Anderson, N. and West, M.A. (1994). *The Team Climate Inventory: Manual and user's guide.* Windsor, Berks: ASE Press.

Applebaum, E. and Batt, R. (1994). *The New American Workplace: Transforming work systems in the United States.* New York: ILR Press.

Bunce, D. and West, M.A. (1995). Self perceptions and perceptions of group climate as predictors of individual innovation at work. *Applied Psychology: An International Review, 44,* 199 – 215.

Burningham, C. and West, M.A. (1995). Individual, climate and group interaction processes as predictors of work team innovation. *Small Group Research, 26:1,* 106 – 117.

Chatwin, B. (1987). *The Songlines.* London: Picador.

Daft, R.L., (1992). *Organizational Theory and Design, 4th edn.* New York: West Publishing Company.

Ford, C.M. and Gioia, D.A. (Eds) (1995). *Creative Action in Organizations – Ivory tower visions and real world voices.* London: Sage Publications.

Hackman, J.R. and Oldham, G.R. (1980). *Work Redesign.* Reading, MA: Addison-Wesley.

HMSO (1993). *Realising our Potential: A strategy for science, technology and engineering* (Cmnd, 2750). London: HMSO.

Kahn, W.A. (1992). To be fully there – psychological presence at work. *Human Relations, 45,* 321 – 349.

Kapleau, P. Roshi (1980). *The Three Pillars of Zen.* Boston: Beacon Press.

Lawthom, R., Patterson, M., West, M. A. and Maitlis, S. (1996). *The Organizational Climate Indicator: Development and validation.* Sheffield: Institute of Work Psychology.

Lewin, K. (1935). *A Dynamic Theory of Personality.* New York: McGraw Hill.

Macy, B.A. and Izumi, H. (1993). Organizational change, design, and work innovation: A meta-analysis of 131 North American field studies – 1961 to 1991. *Research in Organizational Change and Development, Vol. 7.* Greenwich, CT: JAI Press.

Markiewicz, L. and West, M.A. (1996). *The Teambased Organization: A practical guide.* Sheffield: ECITB/Grampian.

Mohrman, S.A., Cohen, S.G. and Mohrman, A.M. (1995). *Designing Team-based Organizations: New forms for knowledge work.* San Francisco: Jossey Bass.

Nelson, D.L. and Quick, J.C. (1994). *Organizational Behavior: Foundations, realities and challenges.* St. Paul, MN: West Publishing.

Nemeth, C. and Staw, B.M. (1989). The trade offs of social control and innovation in groups and organizations. In L. Berkowitz (Ed.), *Advances in Experimental Social Psychology, Vol 2*. New York: Academic Press.

Nicholson, N. and West, M.A. (1988). *Managerial Job Change: Men and women in transition*. Cambridge: Cambridge University Press.

Payne, R. (1990). The effectiveness of research teams: A review. In M.A. West and J.L. Farr (Eds), *Innovation and Creativity at Work: Psychological and Organizational Strategies*. Chichester: Wiley.

Pillinger, T. and West, M. (1995). *Innovation in UK Manufacturing*. Institute of Work Psychology, University of Sheffield and The Centre for Economic Performance, London School of Economics and Political Science.

Quinn, R. E., Faerman, S. R., Thompson, M.P., and McGrath, M.R. (1990). *Becoming a Master Manager*. Chichester: John Wiley.

Rogers, E.M. (1983). *Diffusion of Innovations, 3rd edn*. New York: Free Press.

Rosenfeld, R. and Servo, J.C. (1990). Facilitating innovation in large organizations. In M.A. West and J.L. Farr (Eds), *Innovation and Creativity at Work: Psychological and Organizational Strategies*. Chichester: John Wiley.

Slocum, J.W. (1995). Group culture. In N. Nicholson (Ed.), *Blackwell Encyclopaedic Dictionary of Organizational Behavior*. Oxford: Blackwell.

Van Gundy, A.B. (1988). *Techniques of Structured Problem Solving (2nd edn)*. New York: Van Nostrand, Reinhold.

Wall, T.D. and Jackson, R.P. (1995). New Manufacturing Initiatives and Shopfloor Job Design. In A. Howard (Ed), *The Changing Nature of Work*. San Francisco: Jossey Bass.

West, M.A. (1994). *Effective Teamwork*. Leicester: BPS Books (The British Psychological Society).

West, M.A. (Ed). (1996). *Handbook of Work Group Psychology*. Chichester: Wiley.

West, M.A. and Anderson, N. (1992). Innovation, cultural values and the management of change in British hospitals. *Work and Stress, 6*, 293–310.

West, M.A. and Anderson, N.T. (1996). Innovation in top management teams. *Journal of Applied Psychology, 81(6)*, 680–693.

FURTHER READING

Adams, J. (1988). *The Care and Feeding of Ideas.* Harmondsworth: Penguin.

Csikszentmihalyi, M. and LeFeure, J. (1989). Optimal experience in work and leisure. *Journal of Personality and Social Psychology, 56,* 815 – 822.

Daft, R.L. (1992). *Organization Theory and Design (4th edn.).* New York: West.

Davidson, M. (1996). Women and employment. In P.B. Warr (Ed.), *Psychology at Work.* Harmondsworth: Penguin.

Farr, J.L. and West, M.A. (Eds) (1990). *Innovation and Creativity at Work: Psychological and organizational strategies.* Chichester: Wiley.

Ford, C.M. and Gioia, D.A. (Eds) (1995). *Creative Action in Organizations – Ivory tower visions and real world voices.* London: Sage Publications.

George, J.M. and Brief, A.P. (1992). Feeling good – doing good: A conceptual analysis of the mood at work – organizational spontaneity relationship. *Psychological Bulletin, 112,* 310 – 329.

Guzzo, R.A. and Shea, G.P. (1992). Group performance and intergroup relations. In M.D. Dunnette and L.M. Hough (Eds), *Handbook of Industrial and Organizational Psychology, Vol. 3.* Palo Alto, CA: Consulting Psychologists Press.

Hellriegel, D., Slocum, J.W., and Woodman, R.W. (1992). *Organizational Behavior.* St. Paul, MN: West Publishing.

Henry J,. (Ed.) (1991). *Creative Management.* London: Sage Publications.

Henry, J. and Walker, D. (Eds) (1991). *Managing Innovation.* London: Sage Publications.

King, N. (1990). Innovation at work: the research literature. In M.A. West and J.L. Farr (Eds), *Innovation and Creativity at Work: Psychological and organizational strategies.* Chichester: John Wiley.

Langer, E.J. and Piper, A.I. (1987). The prevention of mindlessness. *Journal of Personality and Social Psychology, 53,* 280 – 287.

Mumford, M.D. and Gustafson, S.B. (1988). Creativity syndrome: Integration, application and innovation. *Psychological Bulletin, 103,* 27 – 43.

Nemeth, C. and Owens, P. (1996). Making work groups more effective: The value of minority dissent. In M. A. West (Ed.) *Handbook of Work Group Psychology.* Chichester: John Wiley.

Noe, R.A., Hollenbeck, J.R., Gerhart, B. and Wright, P.M. (1994). *Human Resource Management: Gaining a competitive advantage.* Boston, Mass: Irwin.

Sternberg, R.J. (1988). *The Nature of Creativity: Contemporary psychological perspectives.* Cambridge: Cambridge University Press.

Tushman, M.L. and Moore, W.L. (Eds) (1988). *Readings in the Management of Innovation.* New York: Harper and Row.

West, M.A. (1987). *The Psychology of Meditation.* Oxford: Oxford University Press.

West, M.A. (1990). The social psychology of innovation in groups. In M.A. West and J.L. Farr (Eds), *Innovation and creativity at work: Psychological and organizational strategies.* Chichester: John Wiley.

West, M.A. and Altink, W.M. (1996). Innovation in organizations. *European Journal of Work and Organizational Psychology, 5:1,* 3 –159.

West, M.A., Lawthom, R., Patterson, M. and Staniforth, D. (1995). *Still Far to Go: The management of UK manufacturing.* University of Sheffield and The Centre for Economic Performance, London School of Economics and Political Science.

INDEX
Compiled by Frances Coogan

Also available in this series

Managing Time
David Fontana

'a well focused little reader.'
NATFHE Journal

Time is one resource that cannot be stretched. David Fontana assists readers to clarify aims and objectives, act rather than react, identify causes of time-wasting and effectively use technology. Exercises and case studies from different professional situations are used throughout to help readers identify and examine unsatisfactory aspects of the way they and their colleagues manage time.

1993; 128pp; 1 85433 089 6 pb;
1 85433 088 8 hb

Coaching for Staff Development

Angela Thomas

Effective managers get work done largely through others; thus the ability to coach is an important skill. Coaching is much more than on the job training or simple delegation; good coaching involves the long-term development of staff and demands good management skills that have to be learned and practised – communication skills, an understanding of different learning styles and a willingness to analyse motives and work practices are required.

1995; 144pp; 1 85433 155 8

Personal & Professional Development

Effective Teamwork

Michael West

Teamwork is now a central strategy for most modern organizations, but it presents many challenges and difficulties, and much of what is written about it ignores the underlying research. This book draws on a wealth of empirical research together with the author's wide experience of working with teams in health care settings, major international organizations (such as IBM and BP) as well as educational institutions.

Michael West is Co-Director of the Corporate Performance Program of the ESRC Centre for Economic Performance (London School of Economics) and Professor of Work and Organizational Psychology (University of Sheffield).

1994; 144pp; 1 85433 138 8

Basic Evaluation Methods: Analysing Performance, Practice and Procedure

Glynis Breakwell & Lynne Millward

Evaluation of staff and procedures is now a regular part of organizational efficiency across the whole professional spectrum. Yet few people are given any training or guidance in how to set about it. This book provides this guidance, giving a step-by-step guide to designing evaluations in your company. Questions of costs, benefits, types of methods and ethics are all discussed.

This book also equips the reader with the skills to assess evaluations provided by outsiders.

Professor Glynis Breakwell is Professor of Psychology at Surrey University and a consultant in industry. Dr Lynne Millward has wide experience in the fields of evaluation, training and assessment centres.

1995; 144pp; 1 85433 161 2

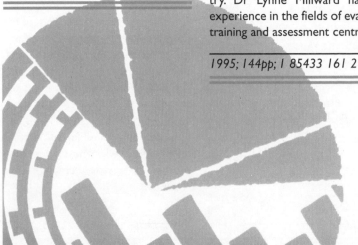

Personal & Professional Development

Interpersonal Conflicts at Work

Robert J. Edelmann

'enables readers to use psychology in a practical way.'
Training Officer

This book examines why conflicts arise and provides strategies for dealing effectively with relationships in the workplace. This is a practical guide with a section on harassment at work and what to do when conflicts persist. It focuses on: rules of relationships, aspects of leadership and gender, personality and age differences, the role of our own beliefs and assumptions.

This is an ideal text for all those experiencing conflicts at work, who want to find out how they can manage their relationships in the workplace.

Dr Edelmann is a clinical psychologist and counsellor in occupational stress.

1993; 128pp; 1 85433 087 X pb; 1 85433 086 1 hb

Teaching and Training for Non-Teachers

Derek Milne and Steve Noone

Every organization must invest in the training of its staff if it is to maintain standards and develop skills in the workforce. This results in a large demand for training, and as specialist teachers and trainers are unable to meet this demand on their own, an increasingly wide range of staff find themselves having to take on a teaching role.

This book is a practical guide for all such reluctant teachers. It offers a thorough and thoughtful guide to the key tasks and skills of training, starting with assessing learners' needs. In addition, it shows the reader how to develop their teaching effectiveness by experiential learning. Exercises, questionnaires and case studies are used throughout.

Derek Milne is Regional Tutor in Clinical Psychology in the Northern Region, and has written extensively about teaching and training. Steve Noone has worked on a wide range of staff training projects. His PhD thesis is on the variables involved in fostering learning.

April 1996; 144pp; 1 85433 184 1